AIRFIX
magazine guide 6

RAF
Fighters
of
World War 2

Alan W Hall

Patrick Stephens Ltd
in association with Airfix Products Ltd

First published – April 1975

ISBN 0 85059 204 6

Don't forget these other Airfix Magazine Guides!

No 1 *Plastic Modelling*
by Gerald Scarborough
No 2 *Aircraft Modelling*
by Bryan Philpott
No 3 *Military Modelling*
by Gerald Scarborough
No 4 *Napoleonic Wargaming*
by Bruce Quarrie
No 5 *Tank and AFV Modelling*
by Gerald Scarborough

Cover design by Ian Heath

Text set in 8 on 9 pt Helvetica Medium
by Blackfriars Press Limited,
Leicester.
Printed by The Garden City Press
Limited, Letchworth, Herts, on
Factotum Cartridge 94 gsm.
Bound by J. M. Dent & Sons Limited,
Letchworth, Herts.
Published by Patrick Stephens
Limited, Bar Hill, Cambridge, CB3
8EL, in association with Airfix
Products Limited, London SW18.

Contents

Editor's introduction

This book has been written specifically for the younger reader who may not have the vast library of books and magazines generally acquired by his adult enthusiast colleagues. It sets out to describe all of the major aircraft types used by the RAF, both British and American, in fighter squadron service during World War 2. In addition one or two aircraft types have been included which significantly added to the rapid growth in technical ability and scientific knowledge needed to keep ahead of an equally advanced enemy.

It is hoped that the simplicity of approach together with some good pictures will provide interesting reading and above all stimulate the interest of the younger reader to go further than just idle curiosity into a period of aviation now more than 25 years old and perhaps a little beyond his understanding.

Being part of a series mainly concerned with model making, it is perhaps heartening that all of the aircraft described with perhaps one exception are now available in plastic construction kit form. Most of these are also in 1:72 scale but several such as the Spitfire, Hurricane, Beaufighter, Mosquito, Typhoon, Mustang, Kittyhawk and Thunderbolt are produced in larger scales.

No attempt has been made to deal with the complicated subject of aircraft markings here, since other books in this series will be published which can more adequately show how colours varied with the theatre of operations and role of the aircraft concerned.

Many books and magazine articles have dealt with the aircraft subjects in this book. Alan Hall has studied all of them in an attempt to get the story accurate and authoritative. Opinions expressed are, naturally, those of the author but were considered in the light of a quarter century of progress in aircraft development and perhaps some of the problems facing aircraft designers today.

BRUCE QUARRIE

Acknowledgements

Although most of the photographs illustrating this book came from the author's own files, grateful acknowledgement is made to Aviation Photo News, Brian Stainer, John Rawlings, Paul A. Jackson, M. J. F. Bowyer, Paul Leaman, the Imperial War Museum and other photo agencies for their assistance.

Prelude to war

The Royal Air Force entered World War 2 ill-equipped to fight on either the land, sea or air fronts. Valiant efforts had been made by the Services and industry to catch up with these deficiencies and it was due to Prime Minister Chamberlain's 'peace in our time' policy that Britain gained a few more precious months in which to prepare.

In 1938, at the time of the Munich non-aggression pact, RAF Fighter Command's main aircraft equipment consisted of outclassed and outgunned biplane fighters. At that time the Spitfire was only just about to enter service with No 19 Squadron at Duxford and there were only two Hurricane squadrons, Nos 111 and 56 with No 85 in the process of converting.

There were only two Groups of Fighter Command, Nos 11 and 12, and these had between them a total of 30 fighter squadrons including the Auxiliaries, made up of Hawker Fury, Gloster Gauntlet and Gladiator single-seat fighters, Hawker Demon two-seat fighters and two squadrons converting to Blenheim Ifs.

Against this background can be seen the results of years of disarmament policy coupled with little advancement in aerial fighting techniques. It will be seen in later chapters that most of the RAF's ideas on this subject were based on World War 1 thinking. The Hawker Demon was a prime example, as this two-seat fighter was a direct descendant of the highly successful Bristol F2b fighter of the previous conflict and its ideals were to be embodied in the Defiant which was one of the early failures of Fighter Command.

The Demon, in its day, however, was a good machine. It came from the famous Hawker Hart bomber which surprised all the pundits, at the time of its introduction, by being faster than contemporary fighters. The design was developed into many different aircraft types, all having the same

The graceful lines of this biplane fighter, the Hawker Fury I, have yet to be equalled by any fighter aircraft since pre-war days.

Hawker Demon of No 604 Squadron when operating from Hendon. The fuselage stripe and wheel covers are red and yellow (Flight International).

configuration. Aircraft such as the Hind, Hardy, Audax and later the Hector maintained the tradition and all except the latter relied on the Kestrel engine.

The first attempts to protect the gunner, seated aft of the pilot in the Demon, were made at this time. Power-operated turrets had only just been introduced into service in the Boulton Paul Overstrand bomber and it was not surprising that, as Demon production was moved from the parent Hawker factory to that of Boulton Paul at Wolverhampton, an attempt should be made to introduce the innovation on their production line.

The design team adopted a Frazer-Nash idea which was hydraulically operated and had a 'lobster-back' shield which protected the gunner from the slipstream and from enemy fire. The turret still mounted a single Lewis gun, but the idea was born, and from that time onward great strides were made — particularly in bomber production where the power-operated turret was essential. Frazer-Nash and Boulton Paul went on to be two of the leading turret manufacturers in the country and their designs were adapted in certain instances into the US aircraft industry.

Perhaps the most beautiful of all of the fighter aircraft since World War 1

and even to this day was the Hawker Fury. This machine, too, was a close cousin of the Hart bomber as it also used the Kestrel engine and had a distinct family resemblance in its design.

It was certainly the most elegant of all of the RAF's biplane fighters as it had a superbly streamlined shape, while in the Mk II version wheel spats were fitted adding even more to its attractive appearance. The original prototype was known as the Hornet and created quite a stir when it was first unveiled at the Olympia exhibition in 1929. The first real Fury flew in March 1931 and a total of 117 were built for the RAF between that date and 1935.

The Fury was undoubtedly the finest aircraft ever used for aerobatic performances. It was also the first to exceed 200 mph in level flight and first equipped No 43 Squadron at RAF Tangmere in May-June 1931. In their public demonstration of that year, aircraft of this unit delighted the Hendon air show spectators by their superb flying, and later aircraft of No 25 Squadron did tied-together aerobatics proving their ability to fly close formation with breathtaking precision.

The Fury II had a 20 per cent increase in power by the substitution of the Kestrel VI for the Kestrel IIS which gave it a top speed of 223 mph.

RAF fighters of World War 2

This produced a much improved rate of climb sufficient to outstrip its contemporaries in Fighter Command.

Even so, the Gloster Gauntlet had the honour of being the last truly open cockpit fighter in RAF service and outlived the Fury by a few months. It was not until the bulk arrival of Spitfires in Fighter Command, which did not take place until the late months of 1939, that this chubby radial-engined biplane was retired from front-line service.

The Gauntlet followed a line of famous predecessors as before it had gone the Grebe and Gamecock, both also equipped with radial engines and two Vickers machine-guns.

At the height of its career in 1937 this machine was in use by no less than 14 RAF fighter squadrons as it came at the time of considerable expansion in the RAF and was the mainstay of the Command until supplanted by Gladiators and later Spitfires. A few squadrons of the Royal Auxiliary Air Force were also equipped with Gauntlets just before the war as an interim measure until more modern machines could be brought into service.

The invention of radar, which was in its very experimental stages before the war, was helped to some extent by Gauntlets of No 32 Squadron based at Biggin Hill. The first ground controlled interception was made by an aircraft of this squadron in November 1937 when it was guided on to the flight path of a civil airliner flying over the Thames. Another Gauntlet, K7810, which had originally served with No 111 Squadron, went to RAE Farnborough to act as a target aircraft to investigate the signal returns on the cathode ray tubes.

Contrary to popular belief, the Gauntlet saw active service during the war and forms the natural link between its well-known period of service and that which followed. Four aircraft were allocated to two Meteorological Flights at Duxford and Aldergrove in the UK and these made daily climbs to above 20,000 feet to check on temperatures and humidity in the upper atmosphere for weather report-

The Boulton Paul-built Hawker Turret Demon. Note that the 'lobster-back' protection behind the gunner provides shelter from both the slipstream and enemy gunfire (Flight International).

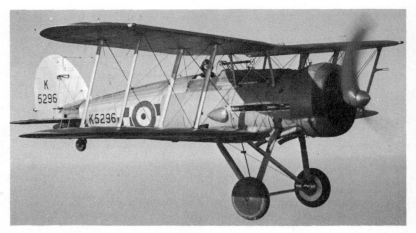

The Gauntlet, this is a No 19 Squadron machine, was the last of the open cockpit fighters to see service in the RAF. Last known service use was in 1943.

ing. The final flight was not made until December 1939 before the Gauntlets finally gave way to Gladiators.

Other than this, Gauntlets served in the Middle East with No 6 Squadron up until the middle of 1940 before the last machine, K5292, was handed over for training duties. The last known instance of Gauntlets on active service was in 1943 when, due to a temporary shortage of Gladiators in East Africa, four were delivered to No 1414 Meteorological Flight at Eastleigh, Nairobi.

Biplane fighters did not have much success during the early war years. Even so, aircraft such as the Gladiator did yeoman service in Norway and Malta and the Italians used their Fiat CR.42 biplanes for many operational sorties in the desert war and even on their few operations during the Battle of Britain. In determined hands the biplane could be used to inflict casualties on enemy fighters and bombers often far superior to themselves in performance and armament.

The end of the biplane era saw the introduction of the monoplane fighter and its accelerated development up to the end of World War 2 culminating in the jet fighter on both the Allied and German sides. The changeover was almost complete and in the case of the RAF a rapid one, for the Battle of Britain was fought entirely by monoplanes except for the Italian intrusion. Techniques, armament and scientific advancement happened overnight and although the RAF had its failures, those aircraft that were developed added more to aviation knowledge in the following five years than had been gained in the previous 20.

Five years' development

When one considers the development of fighter aircraft in the Royal Air Force, or in any other country for that matter, during World War 2, the most important thing to consider is the rapid strides made in technology during those five years.

From a maximum speed of 253 mph attainable by the biplane Gladiator to the 450 mph of the Meteor one can understand the vast step forward in technology that was forced on the aircraft industry in order to keep ahead of the enemy's progress in the same direction.

Speed, and with it engine development, was only one aspect of this advance. The Gladiator, to return to this example, was not far removed from its predecessor the Gauntlet which had an open cockpit ... by the end of the war fighters were flying and fighting at heights of up to 45,000 feet using pressure cabins, far removed from 30,000 feet, the maximum that the biplane could achieve. Similarly developments in armament, range, and electronics kept pace with the demands.

It is therefore not surprising that, faced with these inspiring advances, those directing the use of fighters during the war were given to wrong attitudes in the use of their advantages. The Typhoon was one example. Early versions had a cockpit which was designed without consideration for a good all-round view. It was thought at that time that fighters would make one attack on the enemy and after diving on the foe be many miles away after this one assault, not needing to look round for the attackers on their tails. This deficiency was soon put right in the light of experience as the Typhoon, like the present-day jet fighters capable of speeds far in excess of the speed of sound, still needed to be able to 'mix it' with defending or opposing fighter aircraft. A good all-round view in addition to all the electronic aids now available is

Pre-war shot of a No 3 Squadron Gloster Gladiator at Kenly (Leslie Hunt).

Five years' development

Beaufighter Mk X at RAF Seletar just after the war (R. R. Prior).

Still going strong is this Spitfire PR XIX, PM631, of the RAF's Battle of Britain Flight which provides so much enjoyment at air displays around the country. This machine was built in 1945 and first saw service from RAF Benson (MoD).

still an essential in the design of a good fighter aircraft.

Fighters in World War 2 were transformed from the 'stick and string' era not far removed from their contemporaries of 25 years before to sophisticated weapons of attack. The five years of the war showed how much could be done once the threat was recognised and steps taken to combat it. When thinking of fighters of this period the layman obviously goes straight for the Spitfire and Hurricane, but there were many more fighters worthy of note and this book attempts to set the record straight and bring out the important advances shown in other sectors like jet propulsion which

was only in its infancy at that time.

If one wants examples of this development, the Spitfire is, in fact, a perfectly good case. Like its contemporary on the German side, the Messerschmitt Bf 109, the Spit survived the war from beginning to end but became an entirely different machine from that which fought in the Battle of Britain. More than 20 different versions of this famous aircraft were produced, each having a separate purpose or incorporating some new technology that became available through direct need. High flying, low flying, ground attack, tropical and trainer versions of the Spitfire were built. Although not directly connected

RAF fighters of World War 2

with this narrative, the Spitfire also had its naval version which was also developed from unsophisticated beginnings to continue service for a number of years after the war.

Britain entered World War 2 almost totally unprepared for a long conflict. Although the pundits had warned, re-armament was a slow process, and had it not been for these few far-sighted people there would have possibly been an entirely different outcome in 1940. Hurricanes and Spitfires were, after all, only ordered in quantity three years before 1939, and by the time war was declared only a few squadrons were equipped. In August 1940 the strength of Fighter Command had risen to 19 Spitfire squadrons and 30 of Hurricanes. As was proved this was only just enough to stem the Luftwaffe assault on Britain and only then because Fighter Command was backed by efficient radar defences and the skill based on thorough training by 'the few'.

Elsewhere in the world Britain was even less prepared. The Far East was perhaps the best example of this as the Japanese were able to take Singapore after a desperate struggle by the defenders equipped with almost out-of-date aircraft such as the Buffalo for fighter defence. In the Middle East, the biplane was supreme for some time before new aircraft could be brought from America to provide much-needed support.

The help given by the Americans in supporting Britain's aircraft industry cannot be underestimated. Although the early deliveries of aircraft such as the Buffalo and Mohawk were far from adequate to meet the needs of countering an efficient and technically superior enemy, later deliveries of aircraft such as the Kittyhawk in the Middle East, Mustang in Europe and

Above *Meteor III of 616 Squadron in wartime camouflage* (B. T. Gibbins). **Left** *Line-up of 193 Squadron Typhoons in France towards the end of the war* (Neville Hawkins).

Five years' development

Thunderbolt in the Far East filled gaps which the RAF and the aircraft industry at home were not capable of doing. In reverse, of course, jet aircraft went to America and the advances in engine development made available so that the US could catch up in this direction.

British fighters too had their failures. The Defiant in the Battle of Britain had about as much success as the enemy's Messerschmitt Bf 110 when faced with determined single-seat fighter aircraft. The Defiant followed a theory which arose from the two-seat Bristol Fighter of World War 1 in which the gunner did the fighting and the pilot the flying. Unfortunately this was not the case during the Battle of Britain and although the Defiant was converted for night fighting duties and equipped with elementary radar it did not achieve the success which its manufacturers envisaged.

Similarly, the Westland Whirlwind with its powerful four 20 mm cannon armament did not meet the needs of Fighter Command. This was partly due to the deficiencies of the Rolls-Royce Peregrine engines, though the Typhoon had similar troubles with its Napier Sabre and these were cured. The Whirlwind, although small in numbers, equipped two RAF squadrons. A total of 116 were built and of these most were turned into fighter bombers carrying two 250 lb bombs under the wings. Fighter Command turned the offensive against the Germans by low-level raids across the Channel in 1941, using the Whirlwind, but the aircraft went out of service completely by 1943.

Another fighter design from Westlands was overtaken by events. Designed as a high level fighter to combat possible German machines operating as bombers in these regions, the Welkin suffered low priority in manufacture and other types such as the Spitfire and Mosquito were developed to have the same qualities before it could attain squadron service.

If Britain's day-time fighter defences were poor the numbers of aircraft available for night fighting were even less. The only real advantage was that radar had been evolved so that an elementary and miniaturised version of the successful ground station equipment was ready at the start of the Luftwaffe's night offensive on London. Unfortunately it was in short supply and many aircraft involved in night sorties depended on visual contact and co-operation with searchlights to detect the enemy. The equipment was proved in Blenheims, developed in the night fighter Havocs and used to full effect in the Beaufighters and Mosquitoes that followed on.

The RAF's fighter aircraft in World War 2 provide a fascinating and never-ending subject for research and the detailed description of each type

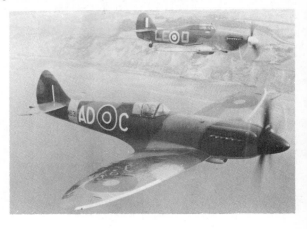

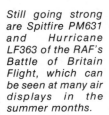

Still going strong are Spitfire PM631 and Hurricane LF363 of the RAF's Battle of Britain Flight, which can be seen at many air displays in the summer months.

RAF fighters of World War 2

that follows is far from complete. An attempt has, however, been made to show the way in which design trends met with operational requirements and were overcome, albeit after some trepidation.

In time of war the pendulum of aircraft superiority swings from one combatant to the other as new developments in aircraft design, engine power and armament are proved. Some aircraft are an immediate success, others take much longer to show their true worth. It is also true that machines designed for one role often end up doing an entirely different task, but this again is often the cause of some requirement at the time and that particular airframe being the only one available for adaptation.

Although all of the aircraft described were used by Fighter Command or its equivalent in other theatres of war they have been divided into their British and American origins. 11 home built products and six US aircraft are described plus two machines, the Vampire and Welkin, which, although they did not make squadron service, are important enough to include in this volume. The Vampire was too late to see action in the war but as its development and prototype form was produced as a direct result of requirements laid down during the conflict its inclusion has been considered necessary to balance the rest of the descriptions given. The Welkin on the other hand saw all of its development during the fighting but was overtaken by events. Even so, its contribution to the knowledge of aircraft development was of considerable importance.

United Kingdom manufactured aircraft in RAF service

Bristol Beaufighter

One of the most liked and adaptable fighter designs on the British side during World War 2 was undoubtedly the Beaufighter. It was originally conceived as a high performance, long-range fighter utilising parts from the Beaufort torpedo bomber. The wings and tail unit were married to a new fuselage and higher powered engines, though Bristols had no direct brief to build the aircraft. Produced as a private venture like the first Mosquito, Air Ministry officials were quick to realise its potential and before the prototype had been completed at Filton, an official order was placed under Specification F.17/39. This called for the completion of the prototype, R2052, plus three others and then a production run of 300.

The design of the Beaufighter had been started at Bristol in 1938 and because of the urgency needed for re-armament the first aircraft was completed within a year to make its maiden flight on July 17 1939. The three other prototypes, R2053, R2054 and R2055 were completed during the next nine months and joined the test programme incorporating modifications as these were found to be necessary. Changes included the repositioning of the engine oil cooler intakes on the wing leading edge, alterations to the undercarriage, and removal of spinners from the airscrews.

Nos 25 and 29 Squadrons were the first to get Beaufighters. One was delivered to each squadron on September 2 1940 during the Battle of Britain and just in time to get into action before the Luftwaffe started its night raids on London. Production meanwhile had been stepped up and three factories, Filton, Weston-super-Mare and the Fairey factory at Stockport were used.

No 29 Squadron flew its first operational sortie on September 17 followed closely by No 25 on October 10. Two more squadrons, Nos 600 and 604, were in the meantime being equipped and both became operational in the beginning of October. The first airborne interception radar-equipped aircraft, however, went to another unit, No 219 Squadron, which received R2059 at Redhill in November.

The first enemy aircraft to be destroyed in combat with a Beaufighter fell to the guns of a 604 Squadron aircraft fitted with AI Mk IV on the night of November 19 1940. This aircraft, a Ju 88, was the first of many German raiders as by now the techniques of night fighting using radar and ground controlled interception were being mastered.

One of the earliest Beaufighters, R2057, having its cannon ports blocked off and retaining the spinners which were removed on later aircraft.

RAF fighters of World War 2

Priority was also given to supplying units in the Middle East with this long-range fighter and by late 1940, 80 had been modified for use in the Western Desert to equip Nos 252 and 272 Squadrons. Range was enhanced by the removal of the wing-mounted Browning machine-guns and extra fuel tanks installed. Beaufighters also went to Malta to supplement the defence forces of the island, operating with No 108 Squadron.

One of the prime users of the many who had Beaufighters was Coastal Command. The Blenheim had previously been adapted as a long range fighter to protect reconnaissance and anti-U-boat aircraft in the Bay of Biscay but it was soon seen that the 'Beau' was better for this task and the Mk Ic armed with four 20mm cannon and six .303 Browning guns created havoc amongst the German fighter forces operating in this area.

Realising that development of the Beaufighter had only just begun with the first aircraft produced, Bristol firstly adapted their design to take two Rolls-Royce Merlin XX engines in place of the Hercules which at that time was needed urgently for night bombers such as the Stirling. The Mk IIF, as the variant became known, served almost entirely as a night fighter in home defence squadrons starting with the first production aircraft R2270 which first flew on March 22 1941. One of the modifications made to this variant, which was later incorporated on all subsequent Beaufighter production, was a 12 degree dihedral tailplane to overcome initial longitudinal instability in the climb. Another general modification was the addition of a dorsal fin extension to cure the Beaufighter's tendency to swing violently on take-off. This was first tried on Mk IIF T3032 and later standardised on the Mk X.

Constant improvements were also made to the aircraft's radar. Originally equipped with double arrow-headed aerials on the nose and wing dipoles, later versions of the night fighter had a scanner, as we know it today, incorporated in a 'thimble' nose. Another idea, this time not successful, to improve the night fighter version was the installation of a four-gun Boulton-Paul turret just aft of the cockpit in a similar way to that on the Defiant. Two aircraft were modified and went to A&AEE for trials, one subsequently being used for a short period by No 29 Squadron.

The next important development was the Mk VI, two versions of which were produced, the Mk VIF for Fighter Command and the Mk VIC for Coastal. Having up-rated Hercules engines, this version, in Coastal service, introduced for the first time a rearward firing Vickers K gun in the navigator's position to give the Beaufighter some rudimentary form of rear defence. The facility was not greatly used by fighter versions of the Mk VI and after a while Coastal aircraft also dispensed with this additional weight.

Perhaps the most significant development in this version was the introduction of the Beaufighter as a torpedo and rocket armed aircraft. The Beaufort had not been the success expected with Coastal Command

A standard Beaufighter Mk I in service with possibly No 604 Squadron. The wartime censor has obliterated the identification of this aircraft on the original picture but the faint outlines of the code NG can still be seen.

strike squadrons and the Beaufighter was therefore developed to take its place after trials at the Torpedo Development Unit, Gosport.

The introduction of the 'Torbeau' also saw the first of Coastal Command's Strike Wings being formed at RAF North Coates in the north of England. Here No 143 Squadron for fighting, 236 for bombing and 254 for torpedo dropping, formed a combined strike force which first saw action against enemy shipping on April 18 1943. Operating together the three units suppressed flak opposition in the initial attack, making way for the low-flying torpedo and bomber aircraft to get into the thick of the action having some chance of being able to place their weapons with accuracy. Combined operations like this sunk many thousands of tons of German coastal traffic in the North Sea along the coasts of Holland, Denmark and even up to the Norwegian fiords.

By this time the Beaufighter had been largely replaced by the Mosquito as a home defence night fighter. The last quantity production version of the aircraft was therefore the Mk X which was supplied to Coastal Command. Equipped with ASV radar and any combination of bombs, rockets or torpedoes, this version was the ultimate in strike aircraft and no less than 2,205 were built. During one period, Beaufighter Mk Xs of Nos 236 and 254 Squadrons sank five U-boats by rocket fire in the Bay of Biscay in two days, more than the entire remainder of the Command's aircraft in a month before.

Mention should also be made of the Beaufighter's service in the Far East. The Japanese called it 'Whispering Death', a title which echoed the success it had in the hands of both RAF and Commonwealth forces, for the Beaufighter was also built in quantity in Australia.

After a production run of 5,562 air-

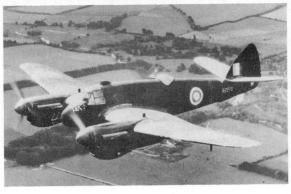

Above *Prototype Beaufighter Mk V fitted with a four-gun Boulton Paul turret and AI radar. Two aircraft were built, this one being R2274.* **Right** *Beaufighter Mk II R2270 illustrates the 12 degree dihedral added to the tailplane of production aircraft when fitted with Merlin XX engines.*

RAF fighters of World War 2

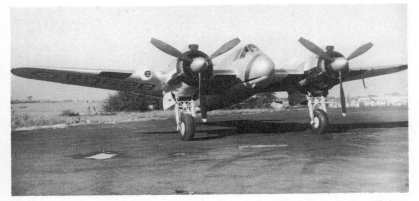

Left *A No 254 Squadron Beaufighter Mk X of Coastal Command seen in May 1945* **Above** *Beaufighter Mk X target tug. Note the yellow and black diagonal stripes below the wings.*

craft the final Beaufighter, a Mk X, SR919, left Filton in September 1945. The aircraft remained in service with Coastal Command after the war and also equipped squadrons in the Far East Air Force until replaced by Brigands in February 1950.

The famous Beaufighter still served with the RAF up until 1960 as many were converted into target tugs as the TT 10 for service at home and in the Middle and Far East. The last operational sortie of a Beaufighter in this role was made by RD761 from Seletar, Singapore on May 17 of that year.

Bristol Beaufighter Mk VIF
Specification
Power plant Two 1,670 hp Bristol Hercules VI or XVI radial engines.
Performance Max speed: 333 mph at 15,600 feet. Range: 1,470 miles. Ceiling: 15,000 feet.
Dimensions: Span: 57 feet 10 inches. Length: 41 feet 8 inches. Height: 15 feet 10 inches.
Armament Four 20 mm cannon in nose and six .303 machine-guns in wings. Mk X had additional .303 gun in rear turret. Provision for one torpedo or eight rockets plus two 250 lb bombs

under wings.

Bristol Blenheim

The Blenheim created something of a sensation when it was first announced before the war. The first RAF squadrons equipped with the type in 1937, and its performance enabled it to outpace its contemporary biplane fighters. Designed basically as a bomber to Air Ministry Specification B.28/35, it was a military development of the famous Type 142 'Britain First' which was presented to the nation by Lord Rothermere in 1935.

The first Blenheim bomber (K7033) flew on June 25 1936. The original contract which was placed in August 1935 called for 150 examples and was ordered straight off the drawing board. The first production aircraft left the factory in November 1936 serialled K7034.

The first RAF squadron to equip with the Blenheim was No 114 at Wyton in January 1937, and the aircraft appeared at the last Hendon Air Display in that year.

In 1938 the Blenheim was adapted as a night fighter under the designa-

Blenheim Mk If WR-E, L1336, of No 248 Squadron at Northolt in 1940. Note the gun pack under the centre fuselage.

tion Mk IF. Over 200 were converted from bombers by the addition of four Browning .303 machine-guns in a gun-pack under the fuselage, and eventually 13 RAF squadrons were equipped with the type.

Blenheim fighters pioneered the use of airborne radar and they came into their own during the night raids made by the Luftwaffe after the main battle had ended. The first successful night engagement came on July 22 1940 and other noteworthy operations by Mk IFs included a raid on the Borkum seaplane base by Nos 25 and 601 Squadrons on November 28 1939 and the first night intruder sortie by No 23 Squadron from Ford on the night of December 21-22 1940.

The introduction of the long-nosed Blenheim Mk IV came in 1939 but these aircraft were mainly bombers, having an extended nose to provide better accommodation for the navigator. Additional fuel tanks were fitted in the outer wings which improved the Blenheim's range and it was therefore considered suitable as a fighter for Coastal Command operating over the Bay of Biscay in late 1940. A similar four gun pack was fitted beneath the fuselage as in the Mk IF night fighter, but the IVF was used almost exclusively for long-range patrol work against the Ju 88s intent on protecting the U-boat lanes out from the French coast to the Atlantic.

Both versions of the Blenheim could be regarded as forerunners of the Bristol Beaufighter. Apart from coming from the same manufacturer, many of the innovations that were incorporated in the later aircraft such as improved armament and AI radar were tried out operationally in Blenheims.

Bristol Blenheim Mk IF Specification
Power plant Two 840 hp Bristol Mercury VIII radial engines.
Performance Max speed: 260 mph, cruising speed 200 mph. Range: 1,125 miles. Ceiling: 27,280 feet.
Dimensions Span: 56 feet 4 inches. Length: 39 feet 9 inches. Height: 9 feet 10 inches.
Armament Four .303 Browning machine-guns in belly pack. One .303 Vickers gun in rear turret.

Boulton Paul Defiant

The Defiant is notable as having been the first and last four-gun turret fighter to enter squadron service with the RAF. It was designed to Air Ministry specification F.9/35 and the first prototype, K8310, made its maiden flight on August 11 1937.

The Boulton Paul design was an exceptionally clean and attractive aircraft. As a pure flying machine it displayed excellent characteristics in spite of the fact that it was slower and less manoeuvrable than its single-seat contemporaries using the Merlin engine.

The lack of speed was undoubtedly caused by the bulk of the four-gun Boulton Paul turret which was installed aft of the pilot's cockpit with retractable fairings fore and aft in an attempt to cut down drag.

The theory behind the use of the turret was that the Defiant could approach an enemy bomber formation from a different angle, knocking down its opponents by concentrated weight of armament alone. The theory was entirely opposed to that of the eight-gun Spitfire and Hurricane but nevertheless the Air Ministry decided to proceed with the design as many remembered the success of the Bristol Fighter of World War 1. It was unfortunate that nobody thought to add forward-firing armament in the wings of the Defiant or else the situation might have been very different.

The Air Ministry specification called for two different aircraft types to be built, the other being the Hawker Hotspur which did not enter service as a fighter though many felt that it was better than the Defiant.

The first squadron to receive Defiants was No 264 which took delivery of their machines on December 3 1939. They first took them into action on May 12 1940 and during early engagements totally surprised the enemy fighters who did not expect to be shot down by an opposing fighter going in an unconventional direction.

The exponents of the turret fighter thought that their theories were justified but the success of the Defiant, even though it shot down 65 enemy aircraft, mainly over Dunkirk, was short-lived. Defiant losses mounted alarmingly and in August 1940 it was decided to withdraw the aircraft from daylight operations entirely.

Whereas the RAF were short of daytime fighters, the night fighter force hardly existed at all. It was therefore decided that the Defiant should become a night fighter aircraft and, equipped with elementary airborne interception radar, it did well during the night raids following the Battle of Britain and had the highest number of kills per interception of any night

Above *Line-up of No 264 Squadron's Defiant Mk Is at Kirton-on-Lindsey in 1940. The aircraft nearest the camera is N1536.* **Left** *Typical Defiant Mk II night fighter fitted with AI Mk IV radar during the summer of 1940.*

Defiant Mk II prototype N1550 at Boscombe Down in July 1942. The deep radiator in the nose stands out clearly and it is also evident that the rear fuselage coaming behind the turret has been retracted.

Defiant TT Mk III, N1697, served initially as a night fighter with No 256 Squadron and later with Nos 288 and 667 Squadrons as a target tug.

fighter type during the winter of 1940-41.

Total production of the Defiant was 1,064 aircraft. These included 713 Mk Is with the 1,030 hp Merlin III, 210 Mk IIs with the Merlin XX and 140 TT I target tugs. The latter used the basic Defiant airframe with the turrets removed and towed targets installed in a bay under the rear fuselage.

As well as this duty the Defiant in its later days also saw extensive service with air gunnery schools at Operational Training Units and with Air Sea Rescue squadrons. It was also tried for a brief period as an army co-operation machine with No 2 Squadron. Production of the Defiant was completed in 1943.

Boulton Paul Defiant Mk I
Specification

Power plant One 1,030 hp Rolls-Royce Merlin III. Mk II — one 1,260 hp Merlin Mk XX.

Performance Max speed 303 mph at 16,500 feet. Mk II — 315 mph at 16,500 feet. Range: 465 miles. Ceiling: 30,350 feet.

Dimensions Span: 39 feet 4 inches. Length: 35 feet 4 inches. Height: 12 feet 2 inches.

Armament Four .303 machine-guns in Boulton Paul turret.

Gloster Gladiator

The Gladiator is well known as the last of the RAF's biplane fighters. It came at the end of a long line of Gloster fighters for the Service starting with such famous types as the Grebe and Gamecock.

All of these aircraft carried on the tradition of World War 1 fighters in that they were of biplane configuration and mounted at the most two fixed forward-firing machine-guns through the propeller. The only advance that the Gladiator had over these was that the armament was increased to four machine-guns and that the aircraft had an enclosed cockpit.

Needless to say the Gladiator was outclassed by Luftwaffe fighters at the beginning of the war but nevertheless did an admirable job in places like Norway and Malta before being superseded by Spitfires or Hurricanes.

The Gladiator was a direct descendant, and in fact an aerodynamic refinement, of its predecessor the Gauntlet. The prototype, K5200, first

RAF fighters of World War 2

flew in September 1934, designated SS.37, and was produced as a private venture. Later, when the Air Ministry issued Specification F.7/30, the Gladiator was entered together with other designs from Blackburn and Westland as well as the original Mitchell design for the Spitfire which had a gull-wing and fixed undercarriage.

In July 1935 the Gladiator was accepted as being the best available to fit the specification although it differed in certain respects from the basic requirement. In order to overcome this the Air Ministry re-wrote their needs into Specification F.14/35 and an initial contract for 23, starting with K6129, was ordered.

So successful did the Gladiator become that a further 186 were added to the order in September 1935 and production continued until April 1940, by which time over 200 had been delivered to the RAF.

Production aircraft had a later variant of the Mercury engine than did the prototype, and later the Mk IIA was fitted with Mercury VIIIA engine, Vokes filter, desert equipment and numerous detail changes. These aircraft served with distinction in the Western Desert starting with Nos 33 and 80 Squadrons in February 1938.

The famous Gladiators defending Malta in 1940 were in fact the navalised version of this aircraft. No RAF Gladiators served on the island

Above *Gladiator Mk I K7985, in the pre-war colours of No 73 Squadron.* **Right** *Pilots of No 54 Squadron running to their Gladiator aircraft in a pre-war demonstration. The Battle of Britain soon taught Fighter Command to disperse their aircraft more than shown in this picture!* (via M. J. F. Bowyer).

UK aircraft

although they were flown by RAF pilots.

Only one flight of Gladiator Mk IIs was in service with No 247 Squadron based at Roborough, Plymouth, during the Battle of Britain. Several other aircraft were, however, stationed at different airfields including the defence flights at aircraft manufacturers' plants and did see some action.

Apart from service in the Western Desert, the Gladiator also equipped the British Expeditionary Force which went to the assistance of Greece when that country was invaded by Italy. Once again the Gladiator was both out-numbered and outclassed by German fighter aircraft when they came to the assistance of the Italians, and it was here that Squadron Leader Pattle won his bar to his DFC.

The Gladiator will be well remembered as a useful aircraft which gave a good account of itself when both out-numbered and pitted against superior enemy aircraft.

Gloster Gladiator Mk I Specification
Power plant One 840 hp Bristol Mercury IX radial engine.
Performance Max speed: 253 mph at 13,500 feet, cruising speed 210 mph. Range: 410 miles. Ceiling: 33,000 feet.
Dimensions Span: 32 feet 3 inches. Length: 27 feet 5 inches. Height: 10 feet 4 inches.
Armament Two Browning .303 machine-guns firing through propeller arc and two additional .303 guns under wings.

Hawker Hurricane

The Hurricane had the distinction of being the first eight-gun monoplane fighter to enter RAF service. It came at a time when Britain's home defence squadrons were weak and the rising power of Germany and its sudden re-armament meant that technology in fighting aircraft had to advance too. Gone were the days of the biplane fighter with its top speed of 200 mph and two fixed forward-firing guns. Gone too, it was thought, were the days of the dog fight in which fighters of both sides 'mixed it' trying to get on to each other's tails for the decisive shot. The former premise was entirely correct but as was seen later, during the Battle of Britain, the Hurricane and its slightly later contemporary the Spitfire, were engaged in equally bloody aerial combat as their predecessors in World War 1.

The Hurricane, although it started life as a fighter was, because of its basically sound design, adapted as a bomber, rocket carrier and, armed with two large calibre guns, as a tank buster. It was a sturdy aircraft built round the undoubted capabilities of the Merlin engine and as a private venture around Air Ministry Specification F.5/34. This was revised following a design conference in 1935 to Specification F.36/34, following which the first prototype flew on November 6 1935.

So delighted with the performance of the prototype were the Air Ministry officials that they immediately ordered 600, which was later increased to 1,000 in November 1938. These were unprecedented figures for peace-time and posed problems for Hawker's Kingston factory to cope within the time limits laid down. Inevitably sub-contracting took place and the Hurricane was being built at several different factories by the time its production reached maximum capacity.

The first Hurricane to enter service was N2423. No 111 Squadron at Northolt was the first to receive them in December 1937, where they superseded Gauntlets. No 3 Squadron at Kenley was the next, and by September 1939 and start of the war, 497 had been delivered and were in use by 18 squadrons.

Hurricane squadrons were the first to go to France with the British Advanced Air Striking Force. Nos 1, 73, 85 and 87 Squadrons were involved and the first enemy aircraft to be shot down by RAF fighters was a Dornier Do 17 which fell to the guns of a No 1 Squadron aircraft on October 30 1939.

The Norwegian campaign saw the dispatch of Hurricanes of No 46

Squadron on board the carrier *Glorious* and another aircraft carrier, the *Argus* was used in the Mediterranean to reinforce the Malta garrison with the Hurricanes of No 261 Squadron. Two squadrons using this aircraft also went to help the ageing Gladiators in the Western Desert, being transported by road across Africa for re-assembly in the Canal Zone.

The Hurricane's main action, how-ever, was in the Battle of Britain. Hurricanes outnumbered the Spitfire squadrons by almost two to one, and as it was discovered from previous combat that the aircraft operated better at lower altitudes where it had a chance against the enemy's Bf 109s, it was engaged primarily on attacking bomber formations whilst the Spitfires concentrated on the protective fighter cover. So successful were these tactics and so great the enemy losses that

Above *Hurricane Mk IIb, the Hurribomber, with two 250lb bombs under the wings, seen late in 1941 flying from Warmwell on cross-Channel sorties. The aircraft is coded AE-W and serialled BE485.* **Right** *Hurricane Mk IIbs of No 601 Squadron on patrol during a cross-Channel sweep during 1941. UF-O is serialled Z3356 and UF-Y BD712.*

on Goering's personal insistence and against the advice of his commanders in the field, the enemy fighters were instructed to stay close to the bombers during the entire operation.

Fighter Command's only Victoria Cross was won by a Hurricane pilot, Flight Lieutenant J. B. Nicolson of 249 Squadron. Other names now famous were made during the Battle by Hurricane pilots. Group Captain Douglas Bader and Wing Commander R. Stanford Tuck being two.

Whilst the battle was going on above them, Hawker's design and production teams at Langley, Bucks, and Kingston, Surrey, were hard at work developing new and more powerful Hurricanes. One of the most important improvements was the replacement of the two-bladed wooden propeller for the three-bladed Rotol unit which added much to the aircraft's power and performance. Similarly the Hurricane Mk II prototype made its maiden flight on June 11 1940 fitted with the Merlin XX engine and two stage supercharger for high-altitude performance. The first to be delivered arrived a mere two months later and retained the eight-gun wing. The Mk IIb meanwhile had been delivered with a 12-gun wing armament whilst further experiments had been conducted on what was to become the

standard wing containing four 20 mm cannon. The first aircraft fitted experimentally with these was L1750 which first flew on May 24 1939. Subsequently the first production Mk IIc was delivered to the RAF in October 1940 and by early 1941 cannon-armed Hurricanes were in the battle.

Other modifications in the ever constant attempt to improve the basic design included self-sealing fuel tanks, tropicalisation for work in the desert and underwing long-range fuel tanks.

In 1941 it was decided to equip the Hurricane with two 250 lb bombs under the wings and the Hurribomber was born. Later two 500 lb bombs could be carried and the first aircraft went into action on cross-Channel raids in the company of Spitfires. No 607 Squadron was the first to use them on October 30 1941 in an anti-shipping raid in the Channel when operating with No 2 Group. Other Hurribombers were sent to the Western Desert in No 80 Squadron markings, some went to Malta and others were sent to the Far East after the Japanese war started.

RAF Hurricanes also became the first and only non-Russian units to operate from Russian soil as in the autumn of 1941 No 151 Wing comprising Nos 81 and 134 Squadrons flew for

RAF fighters of World War 2

UK aircraft

Above *Hurricane Mk IIa, serial unknown but probably a prototype aircraft. Note the unusual open exhausts and consequent staining of the fuselage in the immediate vicinity.* **Left** *Hurricane IIcs of No 3 Squadron. At the time this picture was taken the squadron was changing from day to night fighter duties and was based at Hunsdon, Essex.*

Hurricane Mk IV showing the universal wing with bomb racks for two 250lb bombs. These attachments could also be used for rockets or long-range tanks.

Above *Hurricane Mk IId KZ320 at Langley mounting two 40 mm Vickers 'S' guns under the wings.* **Below** *Rare picture of a Hurricane Mk V having a much deeper radiator, tropical filter and two Vickers 'S' guns under the wings. The four-bladed propeller is also non-standard. The photograph was taken in November 1943.*

UK aircraft

several months from the Murmansk area before the aircraft were handed over to the Russians.

At home the Hurricane IIc became a night fighter and, operating with Turbinlite-equipped Havocs, was responsible for several victories. All-black Hurricanes mingled with normal Fighter Command painted ones on night intruder operations over the Channel coast airfields and even in Holland and Belgium. Flight Lieutenant Kuttelwascher of No 1 Squadron built up an enviable reputation on sorties of this nature.

By the end of 1942 the Hurricane was becoming fast outmoded for fighter-versus-fighter operations. Spitfires largely superseded them in squadron service but that was not the end of the Hurricane as an operational aircraft of great note. It has already been mentioned that the aircraft was adapted for bombing duties, but with the advent of the air-to-ground rocket the Hurricane gained further laurels. The first operation using these modified aircraft was made on September 2 1943 in an attack on the lock gates of the Hansweert Canal in Holland. The aircraft were operated by No 137 Squadron and were escorted by Typhoons, which were later to be adapted for rocket attacks themselves.

The Hurricane also became the first and only aircraft type to be armed operationally with the Vickers 40 mm 'S' gun, two of which were mounted under the wings. Designated Mk IId, this version first saw action in the Western Desert in June 1942 and although the Hurricane's speed was cut to less than 300 mph by the drag of the new weapons, it nevertheless was a powerful weapon in the many tank battles raging at that time. Hurricane IIds also saw service in Burma and one squadron, No 184, had them in the UK before converting to Typhoons.

The last quantity production Hurricane was the Mk IV which was also built in Canada and introduced what was known as the 'universal wing'. This combined all the various roles by then carried out by Hurricanes and provided attachments for either bombs,

rockets or cannon on universal mountings so that these could be attached quickly depending on the type of target to be attacked. The last operational Hurricane squadron in the RAF was No 6 which, equipped with Mk IVs, remained in action in Italy to the end of the war, then moved to Palestine and finally gave up its aircraft in 1946.

The last and final British production Hurricane, a Mk IIc, PZ865, 'The last of the many', flew in September 1944 after 12,780 had been produced in the UK. To this total should be added a further 1,451 built in Canada as Mk Xs, XIs and XIIs.

Hawker Hurricane Specification

Power plant Mk 1 — one 1,030 hp Rolls-Royce Merlin II or III. Mk IIc — one 1,280 hp Rolls-Royce Merlin XX.

Performance Mk 1 — max speed 316 mph at 17,500 feet. Mk IIc — 339 mph at 22,000 feet. Range: 460 miles or 970 with drop tanks. Ceiling: 35,600 feet.

Dimensions Span: 40 feet. Length: 31 feet 5 inches. Height: 13 feet 1 inch. Mk IIc had length of 32 feet.

Armament Mk I — eight .303 machine-guns in wings. Mk IIc — four 20 mm cannon and provision for two 250 lb or two 500 lb bombs under wings. Mk IId — two 40 mm Vickers 'S' guns. Mk IV — any combination of above or eight rocket projectiles.

Gloster Meteor Mks 1 - 4

The Gloster Meteor was the only jet aircraft to go into squadron service on the Allied side during World War 2. The first squadrons of Meteors joined Tempests, Mustangs and Spitfires in the battle against the flying bombs in 1944 and later saw service on the continent.

Design work on the Meteor, which was originally called the Thunderbolt but subsequently changed in March 1942, began following the publication of Air Ministry Specification F.9/40, and the twin-engine layout was chosen because the early jet engines available lacked sufficient thrust with which to produce enough thrust with which to gain an advantage over conventional engines.

Gloster Meteor F Mk Is and Mk IIIs in 1944 being operated by No 616 Squadron. Most of the aircraft in the picture have the Mk III sliding canopy hood but at least three still retain the Mk I upward opening version.

Gloster's first jet aircraft and the first British machine powered by the Whittle W1 turbojet engine made its maiden flight at Cranwell on May 15 1941. Subsequently eight prototypes of the Meteor were built and a production contract for a further 20 machines placed in September 1941.

Most of the early prototypes were engaged in proving the engines and several companies tried out their products in Meteor airframes. The first aircraft to be completed, DG202, for example, when fitted with the Rover W.2B turbojets was only able to make taxiing trials as the engines failed to develop more than 1,000 lb of thrust each. Later another prototype became the first to fly on March 5 1943, powered by Halford H.1 engines, which were the forerunners of the Goblin used to power the Vampire. The second prototype Meteor also flew with Halford engines but the other prototype used various versions of the Whittle W.2 and W.2B. Only one aircraft, DG204, used the Metrovick F.2 axial-flow units.

Manufacture of the Whittle-designed engine was transferred from Rovers to Rolls-Royce and finally emerged as the Welland with 1,700 lb thrust. The fourth prototype, DG205, was the first to fly with these engines

installed and they were chosen as the power plant to equip the first production Meteor Mk I.

This machine, EE210, was sent to America in exchange for the USAAF's Bell P-59 Airacomet, the first United States jet aircraft.

No 616 Squadron was chosen to be the first all-jet fighter squadron when it was stationed at Culmhead on July 12 1944. At the end of that month the squadron moved to Manston, Kent, equipped mainly with Spitfires but with an additional flight of seven Meteors. The move was made to combat flying bombs but early sorties ran into difficulty due to malfunction of the armament. This was eventually rectified but not before one of No 616 squadron's pilots had with great resource flown alongside a flying bomb after his guns had jammed and by a quick flip of the wing-tip forced the bomb down. The aircraft concerned was EE216 and the engagement became the first in which a jet fighter on the Allied side was able to claim a victory. On this same day another Meteor from the squadron claimed a second V-1 but this time using its guns in the normal way. By the time the Germans had given up their launching ramps in the Pas de Calais No 616 Squadron had shot

Meteor F Mk IIIs of No 1335 Conversion Unit.

down 13 flying bombs.

In January 1945 the Meteors of No 616 Squadron moved to Colerne apart from one flight which went to the continent joining the 2nd Tactical Air Force near Brussels. Meanwhile exercises had been carried out with USAAF fighters and bombers emulating the tactics used by the Luftwaffe's Me 262 jet fighter in order that combat procedures, could be worked out to overcome the menace.

The first flight on the continent was later joined by Meteors of No 504 Squadron, the second unit to form, and their first operational sortie was on April 16 1945.

The first Mk III, EE230, had flown in September 1944 and later equipped the squadrons on the continent. The first 15 of this mark flew with Welland engines but subsequently were re-equipped with the new Rolls-Royce Derwent. This was able to develop 2,000 lb thrust and was flown in one of the original prototypes, DG209, in June 1944.

In all over 200 Meteor IIIs were built and they remained in service until several years after the war.

The Meteor III differed from the F Mk

I not only in the engine change but also in having increased fuel tankage and a backwards sliding hood in place of the earlier one which opened sidewards. The last 15 of the latter version incorporated lengthened engine nacelles which later became standard for the Derwent in post-war service.

The Meteor went on to capture the world air speed record of 606 mph in November 1945 and in a second attempt this was raised to 616 mph on December 7 1946. The aircraft was developed into photo-reconnaissance, night fighting and trainer versions and even today several are still flying.

Gloster Meteor Mk 1 - 4 Specification
Power plant Two Rolls-Royce Welland I of 1,700 lb thrust. Mk 4 — two Rolls-Royce Derwent 5 of 3,500 lb thrust.
Performances Mk 1 — max speed 385 mph at sea level, 410 mph at 30,000 feet. Mk 4 — 585 mph at sea level, 550 mph at 30,000 feet. Range: 1,340 miles. Ceiling: 50,000 feet.
Dimensions Span. 43 feet. Length: 41 feet 4 inches. Height: 13 feet. Mk 4 — Span: 37 feet 2 inches. Length: 41 feet 4 inches. Height: 13 feet.
Armament Four 20 mm cannon in nose.

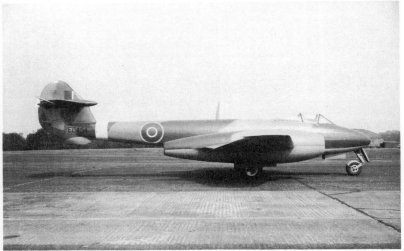

Top *Prototype Meteor EE211/G. Note the early type 'car door' type canopy and the bulbous nacelles of the engines. The photo was taken in March 1944 (via M. J. F. Bowyer).* **Above** *Meteor F Mk 4, EE454, one of the two used by the High Speed Flight in July 1945. This aircraft, named 'Britannia' established a World Air Speed record of 606mph flown by Group Captain H. J. Wilson.*

De Havilland Mosquito

History will doubtless record that the Mosquito was the best general purpose aircraft of World War 2. Whether as a night fighter, intruder bomber, anti-shipping aircraft or high flying reconnaissance machine, the Mosquito adequately filled the requirements in all theatres of war.

From the earliest days the Mosquito was considered as a fighter just as much as a bomber. The original contract laid down in 1940 called for 20 bombers and 30 fighters and the differences between the two marks were small. The fighter version for example had a flat bulletproof windscreen and armament installed in the nose and in place of part of the bomb bay.

The fighter version was the second of three Mosquito prototypes to fly. The first example, W4052, made its initial flight on May 15 1941 and was designated at NFII. It had four 20 mm cannon and Al Mk IV radar. Later, Mk V radar was used and a number of Mosquitoes were also fitted experimentally with Turbinlite searchlights in the nose similar to the Havocs which were at that time having limited success in destroying enemy bombers at night over this country.

A total of 466 NFII night fighters were built and they first entered operational service with Fighter Command in May 1942. First deliveries were made to No 23 Squadron at Ford and No 157 Squadron at Castle Camps. The first operational sortie was made by Wing Commander B. R. O'B. Hoare and by July 1942 No 23 Squadron had been entirely converted to the Mosquito. In December of that year they took them to Malta for intruder sorties over Italy and Sicily.

The success of the Mosquito as a night intruder pioneered by No 23 Squadron led to the introduction of the Mk VI. This version became the most widely used of all Mosquito fighters, the prototype of which, HJ662, made its first flight in February 1943. Two 250 lb bombs were carried in the rear of the bomb bay and two more under the wings. A development of the Mk VI had the bomb load increased plus stations for either bombs or long range fuel tanks under the wings. In all 2,500 Mosquito Mk VIs were built and it eventually supplemented and replaced the Beaufighter as an anti-shipping strike aircraft carrying rocket projectiles in place of bombs.

Coastal Command achieved great success with the Mosquito and one version, the Mk XVIII, was modified to take a 57 mm Molins gun firing a six pounder shell. The first success of this type was made by No 248 Squadron when a U-boat was sunk near the French coast on March 25 1944. Only 27 of this variant were produced but their success was out of proportion to their numbers.

Meanwhile in Fighter Command, Mosquitoes had been employed on long range patrols in support of the bomber forces during night raids on Germany. Mosquitoes attacked defending night fighters on each side of the main bomber stream and on December 24 1943, No 605 Squadron shot down their one hundredth enemy aircraft, over Fassberg.

During the flying bomb raids on England, Mosquitoes shot down 428 V-1s, No 96 Squadron having the highest score with 181.

Several notable raids were made by Mosquito intruder aircraft then operating with the 2nd Tactical Air Force in readiness for D-Day. On February 18 1944, Mosquito Mk VIs of Nos 21, 464 and 487 Squadrons led by Group Captain P. C. Pickard, made their memorable attack on the jail at Amiens.

One of the earliest Mosquito II night fighters of No 25 Squadron. Painted black overall, this aircraft is serialled DD750 and fitted with Al Mk IV radar (via M. J. F. Bowyer).

RAF fighters of World War 2

Above *Finished in day fighter markings of green and ocean grey with medium sea grey undersides, this Mosquito FB VI belongs to No 487 Squadron. Note the underwing bomb load.* **Below** *Mosquito NF 36 operated by No 25 Squadron serialled RL204 when stationed at West Malling, Kent in 1946.*

Bombs carried by the aircraft made a breach in the prison walls resulting in the escape of many members of the French Resistance.

Another attack on April 11 1944 was made by six Mosquitoes of No 613 Squadron which succeeded in destroying the building containing the Gestapo records of the Dutch Resistance held in The Hague. A similar raid on March 21 1945 was made against the Gestapo Headquarters in Copenhagen.

A number of special variants of the Mosquito night fighter were produced. Originating as the prototype Mk XVI bomber, MP469 was hastily converted in September 1942 to combat high flying Junkers Ju 86P nuisance raiders over the United Kingdom. This aircraft had an extended wing span and four cannon in a belly-pack. It was able to reach 43,500 feet and was equipped with AI Mk VIII in the nose.

Mosquitoes did not see service in the Far East until the beginning of 1944. Here they replaced Blenheim Vs in attacking Japanese supply lines in the Burmese jungle.

The last night fighter version of the Mosquito was the NF36 which did not attain production status until the end of the war. Mosquitoes continued to serve in· Fighter Command night fighter squadrons until 1951 when they were replaced by jet aircraft. A total 6,439 Mosquitoes were built in the United Kingdom which, put together with production in Canada and Australia, brought the grand total to 7,781 of all versions.

De Havilland Mosquito VI Specification
Power plant Two 1,230 hp Rolls-Royce Merlin XXI or 1,635 hp Merlin 25.
Performance Max speed: 380 mph at 31,000 feet. Range: 1,205 miles or 1,705 miles with auxiliary fuel tanks. Ceiling: 36,000 feet.

Dimensions Span: 54 feet 2 inches. Length: 40 feet 6 inches. Height 15 feet.

Armament Four 20 mm cannon and four .303 machine-guns in nose plus provision for two 500 lb bombs in fuselage bomb bay and two 500 lb bombs or rocket projectiles under wings.

Vickers Supermarine Spitfire

The first name one thinks of when speaking of World War 2 fighters is the Spitfire. Undoubtedly it was the most potent of all aircraft of its type during the conflict with the possible exception of the Messerschmitt Bf 109 and the Focke-Wulf FW 190. The Spitfire ranks amongst the top three or four weapons on the Allied side which brought victory and can be classed with the atomic bomb, the Lancaster bomber, the Sherman tank and the Jeep.

To write the history of the Spitfire is difficult in the space available in this book so it has been necessary to cut down the detailed description of each mark variant and concentrate on those which were produced in the largest numbers and contributed most to the continued success of the type in every theatre of war.

The Spitfire was designed by R. J. Mitchell and the romantics amongst us would believe that he based much of the Spitfire on earlier designs for the Supermarine S.6B Schneider Trophy winning seaplane. This is probably not strictly true although

Mitchell obviously developed ideas used in the seaplane, which was after all the fastest thing flying in the 1930s, when producing the eight-gun fighter.

The Spitfire was produced as a result of an Air Ministry Specification F.37/34 which called for an aircraft necessitating a design advance hardly ever exceeded since. The fighters of the day, mostly Hawker Furies with a top speed of only just over 200 mph, still relied on theories proven during the previous war, but in the Spitfire the speed was pushed up by 100 mph, the armament trebled, a retracting undercarriage and wing flaps fitted and above all it was designed as a monoplane.

The first production aircraft was delivered to No 19 Squadron at Duxford on August 4 1938. Pilots of this squadron and those of No 66, the second to equip, and also at the same station, took some time to get used to the innovations and there were a number of accidents through their forgetting to lower the undercarriage, and also due to the greatly increased speed available over the Gloster Gauntlet, previously on strength.

The Spitfire, unlike its contemporary the Hurricane, did not go to France or take part in the early war campaigns in Norway or the Middle East. In fact the start of the Battle of Britain saw far fewer Spitfire squadrons in service compared with Hurricanes, due mostly to the longer development time of the former and problems of setting up the

No 19 Squadron was the first to equip with the Spitfire at Duxford in 1938. This picture shows one of the first to be delivered, K9795.

RAF fighters of World War 2

new production line at Castle Bromwich in the Midlands. Spitfires were first committed to action over the Dunkirk beaches but the first enemy aircraft to be shot down by one of their number was a Heinkel He 111 on October 16 1939 whilst attempting to raid the Navy's Firth of Forth anchorage.

During the Battle of Britain RAF Hornchurch became the main Spitfire base. Nos 41, 54, 65, 74, 222 and 603 Squadrons were based there and at the satellite field at Rochford. Because of its better maneouvrability and high altitude performance, Spitfires were committed to attacking the enemy fighter forces during the daylight stage of the Battle. Consequently their losses and the numbers shot down by their guns were less than those of Hurricane squadrons used to combat bombers, and possibly contributed to the controversy that raged as to which was the better aircraft. The fact that the Spitfire eventually reached no less than 24 different mark variants and went on in the Service until well after the war should dispel any doubts on this subject.

One of the earliest photo reconnaissance Spitfires, the 'C' variant seen at Farnborough. Note the enlarged blister on the sides of the already bulged cockpit canopy. These aircraft were basically modified Mk Is fitted with an F.52 vertical camera.

Indeed, it was the Spitfire which made the comeback across the Channel possible. Hurricanes were fitted with bombs and were in their turn escorted by Spitfires in these raids which prefaced the all-out assault on 'Fortress Europe'. The first 'Rhubarbs' were flown by Spitfires from December 20 1940 onward. It was in this period that the first really major improvement, the Mk V, first came into action. Equipped with two 20 mm cannon the new variant was a better match for the current Bf 109s on the Luftwaffe side but not for long. During the summer of 1941 the Germans committed the FW 190 into action and it came as a total surprise to Fighter Command. There was little that the Spits could do against it because the radial-engined fighter was superior in almost every count.

To combat the menace a hurried modification to the Mk V was made by adding greater engine power in the shape of the Merlin 61 and a four-bladed propeller. This stop-gap inno-

vation, the IX, became one of the best versions produced and from 1942, when the variant came into general squadron use, it remained in the forefront of fighter squadron equipment until the end of the war.

One of the earliest subsidiary roles of the Spitfire was in high flying fighting and photo-reconnaissance. As early as 1940 a special Flight of Spitfires was formed to take aerial pictures over northern France and even up to Hamburg. These all-white painted machines were unarmed Mk Is suitably modified, but one of the biggest troubles dogging British designers was an effective pressure cabin. This only became available late in 1942 on the Mk VI, which had a four-bladed propeller and increased span wings with pointed tips. The HF VII followed with a Merlin 61 and it was these aircraft which were hurried into service alongside Mosquitoes at the time of the German Ju 86 nuisance raids on the UK.

The Mk VIII which should have

Spitfire Mk Va fitted with a tropical filter.

RAF fighters of World War 2

The well-known 'Olga'. A Spitfire Mk Vb belonging to No 121 (Eagle) Squadron. Serialled BM590, the aircraft was built at Castle Bromwich.

Above *Spitfire HF VII, high flying version of the Mk IX which had the Merlin 61 engine. Note the extended wing tips of this variant.* **Left** *No 81 Squadron equipped with Spitfire Vbs and operating as part of the Hornchurch Wing are seen here on patrol shortly after their return from Russia in the summer of 1942.*

forces and others went to the defence of Darwin, Australia, followed by the Burma campaign.

Production of the Merlin engined Spitfire ended with the Mk XVI which, like the IX which preceded it, could either be equipped with standard or clipped wings for low altitude work. Using the Merlin 66, the Spitfire XVI stayed in Royal Auxiliary Air Force service after the war.

Mention should also be made of the Spitfire PRXI, another Merlin-engined variant which was used for high-altitude reconnaissance. Fitted with extra long-range tanks, a deepened nose profile and cameras, Spit XIs

replaced the Mk Vs did not see much service with home defence. Most of these aircraft were shipped to the Middle and Far East, seeing service throughout the Desert campaigns and then in Sicily and Italy. Some were active in the Balkans with Yugoslav

This rather unusual Spitfire does not seem to fit into the recognised mark variants. It resembles a Mk V but has the engine of the Mk IX though still retaining the three-bladed propeller. No serial is discernible on the original photo and the background is thought unlikely to be in the UK.

Middle *The Spitfire Mk IX became one of the most important marks of the aircraft. This one, PT465, is awaiting delivery to a squadron.* **Bottom** *Post-war markings of Spitfire Mk XVI RW396 of the Central Gunnery School.*

ranged far over Europe, generally above the heights at which enemy fighters could catch them, keeping an eye on the results of bombing raids and the reconnoitring of new targets.

The Rolls-Royce Griffon engine, which did not reach prototype form until after the start of the war, was soon realised to have great potentiality. Many fighter designs were put forward utilising its power but it was the Spitfire that first had it installed. The prototype of the Spitfire Mk IV was supplied to Rolls-Royce in 1941 and

Above *Spitfire Mk XII, the first of the line to be fitted with the Rolls-Royce Griffon engine, belonging to No 41 Squadron, and serialled MB882.* **Left** *The same Spitfire XII, MB882, showing the underside plan of the aircraft and the clipped wings which characterised the variant.*

was fitted with the Griffon II. Events overtook production and eventually this aircraft was re-designated the Mk XX. Later it was changed yet again with clipped wings to become the Mk XII. Production was given added incentive in 1942 following the daylight tip-and-run raids by FW 190s where an ultra-fast, low-level aircraft was needed to catch them. The version hurried into service was the Mk XII and two squadrons, Nos 41 and 91, both home based, achieved a high success rate in shooting down these sneak raiders.

It was therefore natural that, once the initial requirement was completed, the Griffon should be re-classified as a high-altitude engine and this occurred with the introduction of the Spitfire XIV. Based on a strengthened Mk VIII airframe and a Griffon 65 engine, this version entered service with No 610 Squadron at West Malling and its first duties were to combat *low*-flying V-1s! The aircraft had a top speed of 450 mph and in one case was dived to a terminal velocity of 550 mph, almost the speed of sound. Later versions of the XIV had a 'bubble' canopy and in all 23 RAF squadrons flew them.

Two other Griffon-engined variants were to see service before the end of the war. These were the PR Mk XIX photo-reconnaissance type re-engined from the PR Mk XI and the F Mk XVIII which had increased fuel capacity, a strengthened airframe and undercarriage. A total of 300 were built and saw service in the Middle and Far East until the early 1950s.

After the war several other variants were produced but these are outside the scope of this book. Sufficient to say that the Spitfire kept abreast of the requirements of the war in every way and that once a new threat was recognised the aircraft was happily adapted yet again to meet it. A brief glance at

UK aircraft

No 610 Squadron operated the Spitfire XIV from Lympne in September 1944 during the flying bombs raids. This aircraft is serialled RB158. Note the broader based fin and rudder of this version.

One of the main PR versions of the Spitfire was the Mk XIX powered by the Griffon engine.

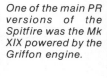

Tear drop canopies were used on the later marks of Spitfire. This one, an FR Mk XIV, also has a long-range fuel tank under the fuselage.

the pictures in this section show how radical the changes were from 1938 to 1945. In all, 20,351 Spitfires were completed of all marks and the last operational sortie of a Spitfire was in April 1954 during the Malaysian anti-Communist action.

Vickers Supermarine Spitfire Specification

Note: as there were so many variants of the Spitfire only two versions, the Mk IX with the Merlin and the Mk XIV with the Griffon engines, have been listed.

Spitfire Mk IX

Power plant One 1,560 hp Rolls-Royce Merlin 61 or 1,760 hp Merlin 66 or 1,710 hp Merlin 70
Performance Max speed: 408 mph at 25,000 feet. Range: 434 miles. Ceiling: 44,000 feet. HF IX — max speed: 416 mph at 27,500 feet. Ceiling: 45,000 feet. LF IX — max speed: 404 mph at 21,000 feet. Ceiling: 42,500 feet.
Dimensions Span: (standard wing) 36 feet 10 inches. Length: 31 feet 4 inches. Height: 12 feet 7 inches.
Armament Two 20 mm cannon plus four .303 machine-guns in wings. IXE replaced .303 guns by two of .50 calibre. Provision for 1,000 lb bombs or rocket projectiles.

Spitfire XIV

Power plant One 1,735 hp Rolls-Royce Griffon III.
Performance Max speed: 393 mph at 18,000 feet. Range: 329 miles. Ceiling: 40,000 feet.
Armament Two 20 mm cannon and four .303 machine-gun in wings. Provision for one 500 lb bomb.

RAF fighters of World War 2

Hawker Tempest Mk V

As soon as it was seen that the Napier Sabre engine of the Typhoon had overcome its initial difficulties a later version of this aircraft was designed by Hawkers to incorporate the new thin-sectioned laminar flow wing which would give it greater speed and manoeuvrability. Elliptical in plan-form the wing could accommodate four 20 mm cannon as in the Typhoon and also have under-wing racks for long-range tanks or bombs. Alternatively an all-rocket armament, but still retaining the cannon, could be used.

Other versions of the Tempest included the Mk II fitted with the Cen-taurus engine but this again led to technical problems and the Mk II did not appear until after the Mk V. Another version, the Mk III, was intended to have the Rolls-Royce Griffon engine but this idea was abandoned.

The first Tempest to fly, HN595, was a converted Typhoon and took to the air at Langley airfield, Bucks, on September 2 1942. The first production Mk V, JN729, flew on June 21 1943 and a total of 800 were produced before August 1945. The Tempest Mk V was the only variant of this aircraft to see war service.

Nos 3 and 486 Squadrons were the first to be equipped with the new aircraft and together with No 56 Squad-

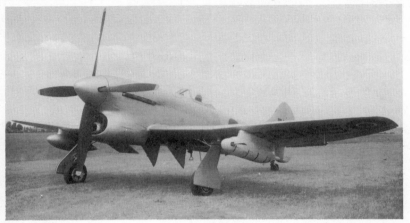

Above *The Tempest was used as a target tug aircraft after its operational service was complete. This example has an all-silver finish and the wind-driven winch on the port wing.*

Right *By the end of the war Tempests were far from clean and tidy. This one, belonging to No 3 Squadron, is travel and battle stained after much service. Note that in 1945 underwing serials, in this case SN161, had returned.*

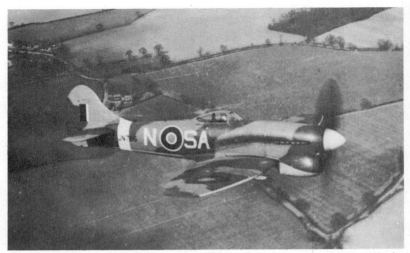

The Tempest was issued to No 486 Squadron in January 1944 replacing Typhoons. This picture was probably taken between then and the following April after re-equipment was completed.

ron formed the first Tempest Wing under the command of Wing Commander R. P. Beaumont at Newchurch, Kent, in April 1944. Their original tasks included interdiction and ground strafing operations in Northern France but the Tempest really came into its own during the flying bomb attacks. As it was the fastest of the defending fighters it also had the lion's share of the total shot down. In all, 638 V-1s fell to the guns of Tempests out of the RAF's total of 1,771 between June and September 1944.

The top speed of the Tempest, approximately 430 mph, also stood it in good stead when the 12 squadrons equipped with the type joined the 2nd Tactical Air Force on the continent during the final assault on Germany. In combat with German jets, Tempest pilots shot down 20 Me 262 aircraft.

After the war, many Tempest Mk Vs were converted into target tugs and some remained in service in north Germany up until 1953.

Hawker Tempest Mk V Specification
Power plant One 2,180 hp Napier Sabre II.

Performance Max speed: 427 mph at 18,500 feet. Range: 740 miles. Ceiling: 36,000 feet.
Dimensions Span: 41 feet. Length: 33 feet 8 inches. Height: 16 feet 1 inch.
Armament Four 20 mm cannon in wings and provision for rocket projectiles or 2,000 lb bombs under wings.

Hawker Typhoon

In spite of a bad start the Typhoon, once it had overcome its teething troubles, went on to achieve great success and add considerably to the art of ground attack which had almost been forgotten since the days of World War 1. The Typhoon became the backbone of the 2nd Tactical Air Force fighter-bomber wings in their advance through Northern France and the Low Countries, developing the technique of 'cab-rank' patrols. Forward air controllers identified targets and radioed their requests to patrolling Typhoons, calling down either one or two aircraft as required to make the attack.

The greatest success achieved by these methods came during the battles at Caen and the Falaise gap when Typhoons devastated enemy motorised units caught in an encirclement movement by Allied forces.

The Typhoon was first conceived before the war. Air Ministry Specification F.18/37 covered a new interceptor fighter which was to be designed round the Rolls-Royce Vulture or the Napier Sabre engine. These power plants were the first to become available using a 24-cylinder arrangement and having over 2,000 hp available.

Most power plants give trouble during their development period but due to the pressing needs of the service both of these were rushed into production before being fully tested. The Vulture powered the Manchester bomber with almost disastrous results whereas the Sabre, after a long period of unreliability, became one of the most useful engines on the Allied side.

Two fighter types were envisaged for these new engines. The other was the Tornado which was designed to take the Vulture engine. This machine, unlike the Manchester, did not get into quantity production and was stopped before development went too far.

The Typhoon on the other hand, having made its maiden flight on February 24 1940, was not without its problems. The first prototype, P5212, was discovered to have a vicious swing to starboard during take-off and bad low speed handling difficulties. Severe vibration was experienced as the slipstream buffeted the thick wing roots owing to the close proximity of the engine and on May 9 1940 the fuselage structure aft of the wing failed for the first time. In addition the Typhoon was discovered to have a disappointing rate of climb and lacked the altitude performance of its contemporaries, such as the Spitfire, already in service.

The first production aircraft, a

Below *This Typhoon of No 486 Squadron shows the earlier type of 'car door' type of entry into the cockpit. Later all Typhoons had a bubble canopy which opened rearwards.*

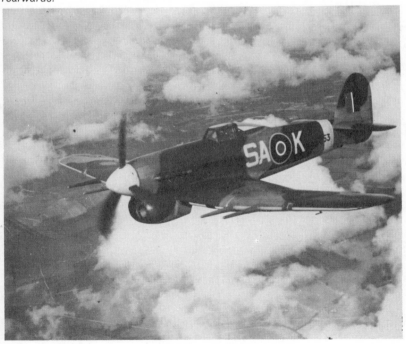

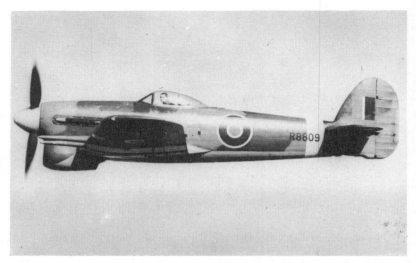

This side view of the Typhoon Ib shows the modifications made to the canopy. A 360 degree all-round vision rearward sliding canopy became standard after complaints about the earlier 'car door' type. Note too that this aircraft has a whip aerial instead of the mast in earlier models (via M. J. F. Bowyer).

Typhoon IA, R7576, flew on May 27 1941 and although the engine and airframe characteristics left much to be desired, first deliveries to the RAF were made in July of that year. The first squadrons to equip were Nos 56 and 609 at Duxford, which received their first machines in September.

At that time hit-and-run raids were being made by the Luftwaffe across the Channel using the Focke-Wulf 190. The Germans had the advantage of surprise, speed and armament over the Spitfire and Hurricane squadrons opposing them. Armed with cannon and bombs they scored a number of successes against coastal targets before Allied fighters could intercept.

The appearance of the Typhoon evened the balance and No 609 Squadron, which started to operate from Manston, Kent, shot down four of their opponents in under a week.

The first Typhoons to enter service were of the Mk IA type which mounted 12 .303 machine-guns in the wings. The more popular version, however, was the Mk IB which had four 20 mm cannon. These first saw action during the Dieppe landings on August 19 1942 and later that year experiments were carried out in which two 250 lb bombs were attached beneath the wings in a similar way to the Hurri-bombers already operating. Three squadrons, Nos 175, 181 and 245, operated in the fighter-bomber role against enemy shipping in the Channel and North Sea during 1943. Meanwhile other Typhoon squadrons were taking part in offensive sweeps over France, Belgium and Holland, attacking enemy airfields and communications. Before long Typhoons had become famous for their 'train-busting' activities and by the middle of 1943 as many as 150 locomotives were being destroyed each month. No 609 Squadron destroyed 100 locomotives in their first few months of operations for the loss of only two aircraft.

Under the leadership of Squadron Leader (later Wing Commander) R. P. Beamont, who had done much to develop the Typhoon during its prototype stage, the Typhoons had other design changes made after they had entered service. For example, the

RAF fighters of World War 2

cockpit of the early versions was entered by a car door type of arrangement. This not only created problems in getting out of the aircraft when it was damaged in battle but also gave a very restricted view for the pilot. A clear view teardrop canopy was later used and the efficiency of the aircraft increased.

By D-Day 26 squadrons were available to the 2nd Tactical Air Force. Much valuable experience had been gained in the months leading up to the invasion by ground attack Typhoons disrupting communications in Northern France.

Most important of all was the addition of air-to-ground rockets to the

Above Typhoon MN173 was used for some time by Napiers for engine research trials. Later it served with No 56 OTU. **Below** Typhoon JP963, coded TP-T, of No 198 Squadron. This aircraft is typical of the period in that it has eight 60lb underwing rockets used to good effect in ground attack work (via M. J. F. Bowyer).

UK aircraft

Typhoon's armoury. It was with this weapon that the aircraft achieved its greatest success. Immediately before the invasion, Typhoons of Nos 198 and 609 Squadrons blasted radar installations at Dieppe/Caudecote and aircraft from Nos 174, 175 and 245 Squadrons destroyed the Jouourg radar station near Cap de la Hague.

As the Allied armies advanced over Europe the Typhoon Wings followed in their wake, frequently changing their bases at short notice. Other modifications to the aircraft around this period included the addition of a four-bladed airscrew to take up the power then available from the Sabre engine. In all 3,300 Typhoons were delivered to the RAF. Production ceased in 1944 and although the Typhoon saw a number of minor alterations, such as a rader equipped version and a photo reconnaissance development, the type was basically unchanged throughout its manufacture. Once the difficulties were overcome of structural and engine failures the Typhoon became very popular with its pilots and was one of

the decisive aircraft in the defeat of Germany.

Hawker Typhoon Mk Ib Specification
Power plant One 2,180 hp Napier Sabre IIA or 2,200 hp Sabre IIB or 2,260 hp Sabre IIC.
Performance Max speed: 412 mph. Range: 510 miles (980 miles clean with auxiliary tanks). Ceiling: 35,200 feet.
Dimensions Span: 41 feet 7 inches. Length: 31 feet 11 inches. Height: 15 feet 3 inches.
Armament Four 20 mm cannon in wings plus provision for two 1,000 lb bombs or eight 60 lb rocket projectiles under wings.

De Havilland Vampire

The Vampire, unlike the Meteor, was too late to see service during World War 2. Its early development did, however, take place during the conflict and it is therefore worthy of inclusion in this book.

Design of the aircraft, initially known as the Spider-Crab, began in 1941 with the issue of Specification E.6/41. De Havillands used the basic

No 247 Squadron became the first Vampire squadron in April 1946. At that time it was operating from Chilbolton. Note the first post-war appearance of squadron badges on the fin of this aircraft, serialled TG301.

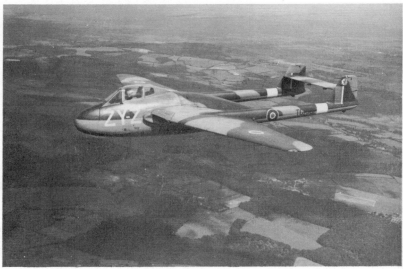

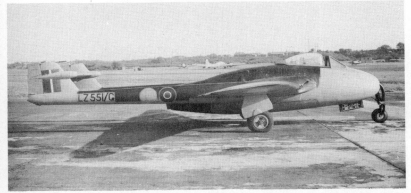

The second prototype Vampire LZ551/G seen at Farnborough during trials. Note the fairing on the tailplane which was deleted from all following production aircraft.

construction techniques that they found so suitable for the Mosquito and the prototype Vampire, LZ548, flew for the first time from Hatfield in September 1943. It was powered by a 2,700 lb thrust de Havilland Goblin turbojet and the initial contract was for 120 machines. LZ548 was joined by two other prototypes, all of which had tall pointed fins. Production versions had these changed to a square cut configuration and the first 40 examples were fitted with the early Goblin engine. After this, subsequent production used the 3,100 lb thrust Goblin 2 and also introduced auxiliary drop tanks beneath the wings.

The first RAF squadron to take delivery of the Vampire F1 was No 247 at Chilbolton.

De Havilland Vampire F Mk I
Specification
Power plant One 3,100 lb thrust de Havilland Goblin D.Gn. 2.
Performance Max speed: 540 mph at 20,000 feet. Range: 730 miles. Ceiling: 40,000 feet.
Dimensions Span: 40 feet. Length: 30 feet 9 ins. Height: 8 feet 10 inches.
Armament Four 20 mm cannon in nose.

Westland Whirlwind

The existence of the Whirlwind became something of a joke to enthusiasts during the early stages of World War 2. Photographs and illustrations giving exact details of the aircraft were released in the German press around this time though the censor had seen fit to keep its existence a secret from the British public. The aircraft was in fact far in advance of its time as, although a near contemporary of the early Hurricanes and Spitfires, it had a four 20 mm cannon armament long before these were considered for use by other aircraft in squadron service.

It was built to Air Ministry Specification F.37/35 and the first prototype, L6844, flew from Yeovil on October 11 1938. The contract was for two prototypes and the second aircraft, serialled L6845, flew shortly after.

The big difficulty with this aircraft was its engines. Equipped with two 885 hp Rolls-Royce Peregrine power plants in finely streamlined nacelles under the wing, it looked an extremely good aircraft for use as a heavy fighter. Unfortunately the engine gave so many troubles in its prototype stages that Whirlwinds did not enter service until June 1940. The first aircraft went to No 263 Squadron at Drem where they superseded Hurricanes. Teething troubles with the engines, maintenance on exposed airfields and a high landing speed caused a number of crashes and it was later discovered that the Whirlwind's performance was

One of the early production Westland Whirlwind Mk Is seen in January 1942.

far below standard at high altitudes.

On the other hand the Whirlwind had a definite superiority at low level and, together with its four cannon armament, offered a greater concentration of fire-power than any other aircraft then available to the RAF.

No 263 Squadron was joined in 1942 by No 137 and the aircraft were modified as fighter-bombers. Sharing the task with Hurribombers, the Whirlwind attacked shipping, locomotives, bridges and harbour installations on the French and Dutch coasts until in 1943 both squadrons exchanged their aircraft for Typhoons. In all the RAF received 112 Whirlwinds, the last, P7122, coming off the production line in January 1942.

Westland Whirlwind Mk I
Specification
Power plant Two 885 hp Rolls-Royce Peregrine in-line engines.
Performance Max speed: 360 mph at 15,000 feet. Ceiling: 30,000 feet.
Dimensions Span 45 feet. Length: 32 feet 9 inches. Height: 11 feet 7 inches.
Armament Four 20 mm cannon in nose. Provision for two 250 lb bombs under wings.

Westland Welkin

During the early stages of the war, the Germans were intent on developing special high flying aircraft for reconnaissance and bombing. The Junkers Ju 86 was modified for this purpose and information on the Luftwaffe's activities reached the planning section of Air Ministry. Conscious of not having any fighter aircraft in the inventory able to intercept these aircraft, a specification (F.4/40) was issued early in 1940 to produce an aircraft capable of attaining altitudes far greater than those of current fighters. Heights specified were over 40,000 feet and a four cannon armament was required.

To meet this demand W. E. Petter and the Westland design team began work on the P.14 which later became

RAF fighters of World War 2

Above *The prototype Welkin Mk I shortly before its first flight at Yeovil on November 1 1942. Serialled DG558/G, it had a taller and rounder fin and rudder than production aircraft.* **Below** *The only Welkin Mk II which was designed as a night fighter and equipped with AI radar. It had two seats and a lengthened fuselage, the observer facing aft. The original serial was PF370 but this was later changed to WE997.*

One of the 67 production Welkins, DX282.

known as the Welkin. A very high aspect ratio wing of 70 feet span was envisaged plus two high altitude rated Merlin 61 supercharged engines.

Progress was slow due mainly to other priorities and the demand for Merlins by the more conventional fighters and bombers then being produced. Problems of an adequate pressure cabin were also encountered and the first prototype did not fly until November 1 1942. Production of the Welkin Mk I began in early 1943 and the first aircraft, DX278, flew in September of that year. A further 66 machines were built.

The pressure cabin was a self-contained unit constructed of heavy gauge metal with an armoured steel bulkhead in the rear. It was pressurised to the equivalent of 24,000 feet at 45,000 feet true altitude and the sliding canopy was of hollow sandwich material to allow for de-icing and de-misting heat to be blown between the layers. It proved to be the first production pressure cabin built for British fighters and although much of the technical achievement was incor-

porated into other existing types during its development, the Welkin can be said to have advanced knowledge of this aspect of aviation considerably.

In 1944 a two-seat night fighter development, the Welkin II, was flown with a much modified canopy and lengthened nose to accommodate AI radar. Only one aircraft, WE997, was built. Events overtook the Welkin and although several of their number were used for experimental purposes none were issued to squadrons. Most ended in breakers' yards before the end of the war. The sole Welkin II was involved in radar development.

Westland Welkin Mk I Specification
Power plant Two 1,250 hp Rolls-Royce Merlin 76/77 in-line engines.
Performance Max speed: 387 mph at 26,000 feet. Range: 1,200 miles. Ceiling: 44,000 feet.
Dimensions Span: 70 feet 4 inches. Length: 41 feet 7 inches. Height: 15 feet 9 inches.
Armament: Four 20 mm cannon in nose.

RAF fighters of World War 2

section two

United States manufactured aircraft in RAF service

Bell Airacobra

The Airacobra was an unconventional aircraft. It had its Allison engine behind the pilot, the power being transmitted to the propeller through an extension shaft, and it had a tricycle undercarriage. Another innovation was the mounting of a 20 mm cannon firing through the propeller hub.

The Airacobra was amongst the first of the many American manufactured aircraft to enter service in the RAF. Due to the collapse of France an order placed before the war by the French Air Force was taken over by the British Direct Purchase Commission in 1940. The aircraft had also been ordered for the USAAC where it entered service as the P-39D in February 1941.

First imports arrived in England in July 1941 and these machines went to Air Fighting Development Unit, Duxford. In September 1941 No 601 Squadron converted to the type from Hurricanes.

In a blaze of publicity (by wartime standards) No 601's Airacobras were heralded into service. Early misgivings about the type led to their being restricted to the ground attack role and indeed a few operations were undertaken starting on October 9 1941 against the enemy-occupied French coast but the aircraft was withdrawn from service the following December.

The RAF never liked the Airacobra due, it was said, to its bad servicability. In spite of this the USAAF and the Russian forces used them extensively. In the later stages of the war Airacobras were serving in the Mediterranean Allied Air Forces with French squadrons of No 340 Wing and with Air Headquarters, Malta, mainly on reconnaissance duties.

The RAF order was for 675 machines starting with AH507 but after its brief operational career,

An Airacobra of No 601 Squadron at Matlaske, Norfolk, before the addition of code markings. This was the only squadron equipped with the type but gave them up after a few operational sorties in March 1942.

deliveries were cut back to about 80, the remainder going to the US Army.

No 601 Squadron re-equipped with Spitfires and their Airacobras were placed in storage. These were shipped to Russia in 1942 with the exception of a few examples which remained on charge with various trials units such as the Air Fighting Development Unit and A&AEE Boscombe Down. The last surviving Airacobra in the UK was AH574 which was struck off charge some time after 1947 after having been used for carrier deck landing trials at Farnborough.

Bell Airacobra Mk I Specification
Power plant One Allison V-1710-E4 in-line engine of 1,150 hp.
Performance Max speed: 358 mph at 15,000 feet. Range: 1,098 miles. Ceiling: 35,000 feet.
Dimensions Span: 34 feet. Length: 34 feet 2 inches. Height: 9 feet 3 inches.

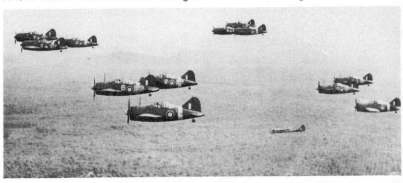

Above *A squadron of 12 Buffalos accompanied by a lone Blenheim IV over Singapore shortly before the start of hostilities in the Far East.* **Below** *A propaganda picture issued just before the start of the Far East war showing a line-up of at least 24 Buffalos, probably at Singapore.*

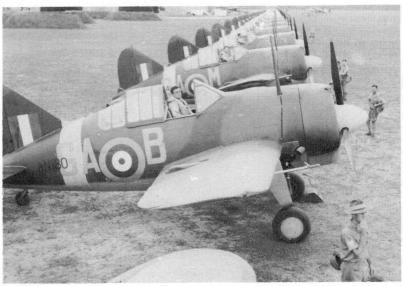

Armament One 20 mm cannon firing through propeller boss plus two .303 machine-guns in nose and four in wings

Brewster Buffalo

The Brewster F2A-1 was first produced for the US Navy in 1939 after the prototype had flown a year earlier. The British Purchasing Commission decided to order a limited quantity as a land fighter for the RAF and placed an order for 180, naming it the Buffalo.

The RAF version was the same as the US Navy's F2A-2 or Brewster Model 339. A Belgian order for 38 of a slightly later version of this aircraft was taken over by the British following the invasion of Belgium which meant that the aircraft could not enter service as intended.

The first aircraft for Britain, W8131, and the first 'Belgian' aircraft, AS410, arrived in England in 1940. They were assembled at Burtonwood, Lancs, and initial deliveries were made to No 71 Squadron at Church Fenton. Trials were disappointing and the aircraft not considered suitable for operational use in Fighter Command.

All deliveries were therefore diverted to the Far East and the Buffalo became the standard day fighter for the four squadrons defending Singapore. These were Nos 67, 243, 453 and 488. The Royal Australian Air Force also had a squadron, No 21, equipped with the Buffalo in this area.

In the event the Buffalo was hopelessly outclassed by contemporary Japanese fighters and although they put up a gallant struggle were easily defeated. The Buffalo had a short and not very successful RAF career.

Brewster Buffalo Mk I Specification
Power plant One 1,200 hp Wright Cyclone GR-1820-G205A radial engine.
Performance Max speed: 313 mph at 13,500 feet. Range: 650 miles. Ceiling: 30,500 feet.
Dimensions Span: 35 feet. Length: 26 feet. Height: 12 feet 1 inch.
Armament Four .50 calibre machine-guns, two in fuselage, two in wings.

Douglas Havoc

The Douglas Havoc was developed from the DB-7 produced by this American manufacturer for service in the French Air Force at the beginning of the war. Much of the contract was taken over by the British Purchasing Commission who subsequently ordered more for use as a light bomber.

On arrival in England 100 Boston IIs were converted into Havocs at the Burtonwood Aircraft Repair Depot, near Liverpool, during 1940-41.

Douglas Havoc NF Mk II in October 1941. This aircraft had a longer nose than the Mk I in which 12 .303 machine-guns were fitted.

With the addition of airborne interception radar, additional armour plating and an eight-gun nose, the first Havoc I, BJ463, was delivered for service in December 1940.

It was painted overall matt-black and had flame damper exhausts. Certain of the Havocs remained with their glazed nose in common with the bomber version but these were later modified and most had large searchlights fitted with which it was intended to illuminate enemy bombers for the benefit of accompanying night fighters, whose job it was to shoot them down. These searchlights, known as Turbinlites, were to equip 31 Havoc I and 39 Havoc II aircraft. The latter, in its pure fighter version, had the nose gun armament increased to 12 .303 machine-guns and was later used for night intrusion over France. Some of the original transparent nose versions of the Havoc were also used for this work mainly operated by No 23 Squadron at Ford.

The base for the Turbinlite night fighters was at Hunsdon, Essex and West Malling, Kent. On operational sorties they were accompanied by Hurricanes which attacked enemy aircraft after they had been illuminated by the searchlight.

Other versions, mainly delivered to No 93 Squadron at Middle Wallop, carried small aerial mines in the bomb bay which were dropped in the path of hostile bombers. The 20 aircraft so modified were not successful and the unit disbanded in 1941.

The final operational variant of the Havoc was a version of the Boston III which carried a gun-pack under the fuselage and was used for night intruder work. It equipped Nos 418 and 605 Squadrons in the summer of 1942.

Douglas Havoc Mk I Specification
Power plant Two 1,200 hp Pratt and Whitney Twin Wasp S3C4-G radial engines.
Performance Max speed: 295 mph at 13,000 feet. Range: 1,000 miles. Ceiling: 26,000 feet.
Dimensions Span: 61 feet 4 inches. Length: 47 feet. Height: 15 feet 10 inches.

Armament Eight .303 machine-guns mounted in nose plus optional mounting of one .303 machine-gun in rear cockpit. Mk II had provision for 12 .303 guns in nose. Intruder version had four .303 machine-guns in nose and provision for light bomb load.

North American Mustang

Although much emphasis is given to international co-operation in the production of both civil and military aircraft in recent years, the North American Mustang can be described as the forerunner of this achievement.

The British Government sent an Air Commission to the United States in April 1938 to explore the possibilities of buying military aircraft. American manufacturers had become leaders in certain techniques of metal airframe construction and after a tour of the major airframe and engine firms in the States, the British Commission found a number of aircraft which they thought would suit their needs. North American at that time were beginning to build the AT-6 Harvard. The Commission ordered a large number and North American were immediately in the big league as far as aircraft manufacture was concerned and their factory at Inglewood, California, looked like having full order books for some time to come.

After the start of the war the British Commission returned under the direction of Sir Henry Self charged with buying numbers of combat aircraft to supplement production from British factories.

Orders were placed for the P-40 but this aircraft was not as good as the contemporary British Hurricanes or Spitfires. North American proposed constructing a single-seater fighter around the same Allison engine used by the P-40 but of a superior design having an extremely low drag airframe. After original design studies, an order was placed for construction of a prototype. This was designated NA-73X and from the start of construction to roll out was only 100 days. The first flight took place on October 26 1940

Top *The fourth production Mustang for the RAF, AG348, seen without armament before being crated for delivery to the RAF.* **Above** *Mustangs were delivered to the Burtonwood, Lancs, repair and maintenance depot where they were assembled and flight tested before being delivered to squadrons. This picture was taken in November 1941 and also shows a number of Bostons on the same airfield.*

and after minor adjustments the Mustang went into production on a large scale.

Although the prototype NA-73X crashed, the work did not stop and North American estimated that the 620 machines ordered would keep them in business for at least three years.

The first production aircraft was AG345 and flew during the last week of April 1941. The whole programme had been completed in less than a year.

One of the innovations on the Mustang was the laminar-flow wing which cut down drag and gave the aircraft a superior performance to its contemporaries equipped with the same engine. First Mustangs reached the UK in November 1941 and despite its

US aircraft

poor performance at high altitudes the Mks I and II went into service, supplanting Tomahawks in Army Co-operation Command Squadrons.

The first Mustang-equipped unit was No 2 Squadron at Sawbridgeworth in April 1942 and it made its first operational sortie in July of that year. Fitted with an oblique camera behind the pilot on the port side, Mustangs were involved in cross-Channel sweeps attacking ground targets as well as taking photographs. The early versions of the aircraft went on to do yeoman service throughout the war and in fact one, AG346, the second Mustang to be built, operated with No 168 Squadron to the end.

Surprisingly the USAAC did not take an immediate interest in the Mustang. They did, however, order a limited number of these aircraft as dive-bombers under the designation A-36 which saw service in North Africa.

It was at this point that reverse lease-lend came into action and the co-operation between British and American designers produced the later marks of Mustang for the RAF and the P-51 for the USAAF. Because of the poor performance of the Allison engine at altitude, the Mustang required more 'poke'. The original

move came from Rolls-Royce test pilot Ronald Harker, who thought that the aerodynamically clean airframe of the Mustang would do well if fitted with the superior engine of the Spitfire. Calculations suggested that a top speed of 441 mph, or more than 70 mph faster than the existing machine, might be achieved. Eventually a Merlin 65 was added to a Mustang airframe which had a fuel injection carburettor and supercharger. The first flight was made on October 13 1942 and the RAF ordered it shortly afterwards.

The USAAF's P-51B and C were the equivalent of the RAF's Mk III. The Mk IV was the same as the P-51D. Early Mustang IIIs had the original type of upward-hinging cockpit canopy, but on later models a bulged Spitfire-type backward sliding one was introduced, becoming known as the 'Malcolm' hood. This again was at the suggestion of British designers and was subsequently accepted by the Americans. The Mustang IV had a moulded bubble canopy which offered improved all-round vision for the pilot. All Merlin-engined Mustangs had four-bladed propellers to take the increased power.

The first Mustang IIIs in RAF service went to No 19 Squadron at Ford in

A standard Mustang Mk I, AM148.

RAF fighters of World War 2

Above *One of the several experiments to improve the already good range of the Mustang was the addition of these peculiarly shaped underwing fuel tanks.*
Below *Malcolm hood Mustang. This Mk III, FB201, belonged to No 19 Squadron when stationed at Gravesend in April 1944.*

February 1944. They were used to escort bomber formations and later went to France with the 2nd Tactical Air Force, flying fighter-bomber operations.

Mustangs were in the lead when shooting down flying bombs over southern England and a total of 232 V-1s were destroyed by September 1944 by these aircraft.

The Mustang's long range, high performance and heavy armament made it one of the outstanding fighters of World War 2. The fact that the USAAF took over what was originally a joint design between the British and North American was to their credit, once the aircraft had been re-engined with the Merlin. The Mustang was without doubt one of the war-winners as far as fighter aircraft was concerned.

North American Mustang Mk III
Specification
Power plant One 1,680 hp Packard Merlin V-1650-7 in-line engine.

Performance Max speed: 442 mph at 24,500 feet. Range: 950 miles (max) 1,710 miles. Ceiling: 42,500 feet.
Dimensions Span: 37 feet. Length: 32 feet 3 inches. Height: 8 feet 8 inches.
Armament Four .50 calibre machine-guns and 1,000 lb bombs.

Curtiss Tomahawk/Kittyhawk

The Curtiss fighters were amongst the first to be bought by the British Direct Purchasing Commission for use in the RAF. Before the war orders were placed for the Mohawk, which was a

Below *This side view of Tomahawk I AH789 was probably taken shortly after the aircraft was delivered to No 268 Squadron and before the application of squadron markings* (via M. J. F. Bowyer). **Bottom** *Curtiss Tomahawk IIb photographed in October 1942.*

RAF fighters of World War 2

Top *One of the first Kittyhawk Mk Is to be delivered seen at Boscombe Down.*
Above *The Allison-powered Kittyhawk Mk IV.*

radial-engined fighter then in service with the USAAF and being exported to Britain's ally, France. Only a few of these aircraft were delivered before the French capitulated in 1940 and eventually the RAF took delivery of 100 examples. These started with AR630 and reached England between July and September 1940. They saw no action in Western Europe but by the end of 1941 had been sent to India and the Middle East. For a period, eight Mohawks comprised the sole fighter defence of North East India and they

Kittyhawk IV, probably in Italy, taxies along the PSP planking with three 250lb bombs on board for a ground attack mission (via M. J. F. Bowyer).

were operational on the Burma front until December 1943. The first unit to be equipped in that theatre was No 5 Squadron which received its first aircraft in January 1942.

In the main, the Mohawk was not a successful fighter as far as the RAF was concerned. Its successor, the Tomahawk, used the Allison in-line engine and was known as the P-40 in American service. Again it was ordered by the French but none were delivered and these were taken over by the British and added to their own order. Almost 900 were delivered to the RAF and saw service with British and Canadian squadrons at home and became the mainstay of fighter offensive operations in the Middle East. Aircraft of this type were also delivered to South African and Australian squadrons.

The first Tomahawk I, AH741, was delivered in late 1940, being shipped to England in crates and erected by Maintenance Units before delivery to squadrons. The first unit to be so equipped was No 2 Squadron at Sawbridgeworth in August 1941, and the Tomahawk superseded the Lysander in low-level reconnaissance.

The Tomahawk's engine was not suitable for high-altitude performance and therefore these aircraft were used for reconnaissance sorties over the north of France, providing much-needed information before operations such as that at Dieppe and the later invasion of Europe were mounted.

The first Desert Air Force Squadron to be equipped with the Tomahawk was No 112, which received them in place of Gladiators in October 1941. This unit became famous because it was one of the first to adopt the 'shark's tooth' insignia on its engine cowling. Eventually home-based squadrons of Tomahawks were superseded by Mustangs and in the Western Desert by the Kittyhawks from April 1942 onwards.

The Curtiss P-40D was the last of the line to see service. Known as the Warhawk in USAAF service, it was used exclusively by the RAF in the Mediterranean theatre, first in the Western Desert, and later in Sicily and Italy. Aircraft of this type were also used by the RAAF and the RNZAF in the Pacific.

Three versions of Kittyhawk saw service with the RAF and over 1,500

RAF fighters of World War 2

were delivered. Out of these, the Mk III was the most numerous and was used as a light bomber, sometimes being called on to fly up to four sorties a day in answer to Army calls for close support.

It differed from its predecessors in having an up-rated Allison engine in the Mk IA and then a Packard-built version of the Rolls-Royce Merlin in the Kittyhawk II. Additionally the cockpit canopy was redesigned and the armament of four .50 calibre machine-guns in the wings was increased to six in later versions. It could carry one 500 lb bomb beneath the fuselage and two 250 lb bombs below the wings.

Above The Kittyhawk was widely used by Commonwealth forces during the war, as this shot of machines from No 15 Fighter Squadron, RNZAF, at Whenuapal in 1942 shows. **Below** One of the few Thunderbolts delivered to the RAF to reach the United Kingdom. Here KJ299 shows clearly the Mk II's bubble canopy and fuselage and underwing bomb racks.

US aircraft

Bubble-canopy Thunderbolt of 60 Squadron at Kemajoran Airfield, Batavia.

The Kittyhawk was extremely well liked by its crews and proved itself to be a sturdy aircraft capable of taking much battle damage. In co-operation with Hurricane fighter bombers, Kittyhawks created havoc amongst Rommel's desert armies and later greatly assisted in softening up targets in the advance through Sicily and Italy.

Curtiss Tomahawk Mk IIb Specification
Power plant One 1,090 hp Allison V-1710-C-15 in-line engine.
Performance Max speed: 328 mph at 15,000 feet. Range: 945 miles. Ceiling: 35,000 feet.
Dimensions Span: 37 feet 3 inches. Length: 31 feet 8 inches. Height: 10 feet 7 inches.
Armament Six .303 machine-guns, two in fuselage and four in wings.

Curtiss Kittyhawk II Specification
Power plant One 1,300 hp Packard Merlin V-1650-1 in-line engine.
Performance Max speed: 320 mph at 5,000 feet. Range: 700 miles. Ceiling: 34,400 feet.
Dimensions Span: 37 feet 4 inches. Length: 33 feet 4 inches. Height: 10 feet 7 inches.

Armament Six .50 calibre machine-guns in wings plus provision for one 500 lb and two 100 lb bombs under fuselage and wings.

Republic Thunderbolt

Although one of the leading American fighters of World War 2, the Thunderbolt did not enter operational service with the RAF until September 1944. It was then used exclusively in South East Asia against the Japanese and equipped 16 squadrons operating on the Burma front.

Known as the P-47 in the USAAF, the original Thunderbolt was developed from the P-35 and P-43. It first flew on May 6 1941 and was the largest and heaviest single-engined fighter to enter service in any of the combatant nations.

Two versions differing in external shape were in general service. The first, known to the RAF as the Mk I, was the equivalent of the USAAF's P-47B and had the original framed cockpit hood. The Mk II was the more widely used version and had the 'teardrop' moulded canopy which gave a

360 degree all-round view.

The first unit in Burma to equip with the Thunderbolt was No 5 Squadron which had previously flown Mohawks and Hurricanes.

The Thunderbolt was used as a fighter-bomber in the same way that the Typhoon operated in Europe. Aircraft flew close support missions controlled by ground posts under the direction of Forward Air Controllers. Equipped with three 500 lb bombs and eight .50 calibre machine-guns, Thunderbolts flew 'cab rank' patrols attacking Japanese troops and strong points as directed.

In all 826 Thunderbolts served with the RAF but these were returned to the US shortly after VJ-Day.

Republic Thunderbolt Mk II
Specification
Power plant One 2,300 hp Pratt and Whitney Double Wasp R-2800-59 radial engine.

Performance Max speed: 427 mph. Range: 1,030 miles (max) 1,970 miles. Ceiling: 36,500 feet

Dimensions Span: 40 feet 9 inches. Length: 36 feet 2 inches. Height. 12 feet 8 inches.

Armament Eight .50 calibre machine-guns in wings and provision for 2,000 lb bombs.

Bibliography

Aircraft of the Royal Air Force since 1918, by Owen Thetford. Putnam.
British Fighters of World War 2, by Francis K. Mason. Hylton Lacy.
Warplanes of the Second World War — Fighters, Vol 2, by William Green. Macdonald.
Janes All the Worlds Aircraft, 1938, 1939, 1940, 1941, 1942, 1943, 1944 and 1945. Sampson Low.
De Havilland Aircraft since 1915, by A. J. Jackson. Putnam.
The British Fighter since 1912, by Peter Lewis. Putnam.
British Military Aircraft Serials, by Bruce Robertson. Ian Allan.
Hawker Aircraft since 1920, by Francis K. Mason. Putnam.
Vickers Aircraft since 1908, by C. F. Andrews. Putnam.
Bristol Aircraft since 1910, by C. H. Barnes. Putnam.
Gloster Aircraft since 1917, by D. N. James. Putnam.
Fighting Colours: RAF Fighter Camouflage and Markings, 1937-1975, by Michael J. F. Bowyer. Patrick Stephens.
Classic Aircraft No 1 Spitfire, by Roy Cross and Gerald Scarborough. Patrick Stephens.
Classic Aircraft No 3 P-51 Mustang, by Roy Cross and Gerald Scarborough in collaboration with Bruce Robertson. Patrick Stephens.
Classic Aircraft No 4 Hawker Hurricane, by Bruce Robertson and Gerald Scarborough. Patrick Stephens.
Profile Publications Nos 7, 8, 24, 35, 41, 52, 78, 81, 93, 98, 100, 111, 117, 136, 137, 165, 166, 191, 197, 206, 209 and 218.
Magazines — Aeroplane Spotter, Air Pictorial, Airfix Magazine, RAF Flying Review, Air International, Aeroplane Monthly, Aircraft Illustrated, Aviation News.